Ann Humphreys

THE TAO OF HOOP

On the Transformational
Practice of Hula-Hooping

(Seriously, Though)

PRINT: 978-1-7376398-0-0
EBOOK: 978-1-7376398-1-7
AUDIOBOOK: 978-1-7376398-2-4

Some names have been changed to protect privacy.

IN MEMORIAM

James E. Humphreys, Jr.
Kimowan Metchewais
Burning Dan Gordon-Levitt

and for
Tommie

Philosophy is written in this grand book—I mean the universe—which stands continually open to our gaze, but it cannot be understood unless one first learns to comprehend the language in which it is written. It is written in the language of mathematics, and its characters are triangles, circles, and other geometric figures, without which it is humanly impossible to understand a single word; without these, one is wandering about in a dark labyrinth.

— GALILEO

God is an infinite sphere, whose center is everywhere and circumference nowhere.

— LIBER PHILOSOPHORUM XXIV

The Point

The way to do is to be.

— LAO TZU

This is one of those goofy spiritualesque self-help-ish memoir books written by some overeducated weirdo still living in a college town. The reason this book exists is that the hula-hoop changed my life. The hula-hoop changed my life because it taught me how to feel. It taught me how to feel through its insistently concrete touch on my body at the place where its form found rotation in relationship to my body's sense of the forces that shape spacetime. It taught me that *feeling* (a phenomenon I experience within and throughout my body) and *thought* (the act of speaking about such experiences to myself) are not one in the same thing. I had never understood that before. I was 36 years old.

The hula-hoop taught me through the place where it touched my body: a distinct ovoid patch of polypropylene along the hoop's inner wall that certain old-school hoopers call the *Point*. The Point of the hoop is the place where it is in active, revolving contact with a living, moving human body.

Through repeated interaction with the hoop's Point, a hooper may derive an evolvingly accurate awareness of the position—at any given moment—of both the entire hoop and the entire body. And through continued practice, across weeks and months and years, a hooper may find herself in possession of an entirely new metaphor through which to perceive the immense flowing implausibility into which she has—out of all the infinite things that could ever be imagined to be possible—been born.

Luckily, there is no reason for you or anyone to take this book seriously on any level, because I have already established that I am a loony, intense, oversharing circus freak who actually believes that dancing with a plastic ring significantly illuminated the meaning behind the philosophy called Taoism—a philosophy I needed very desperately, despite being fully ignorant of this need for the first half of my adult life. I was ignorant because I hated religion. I hated religion because I had lost mine. And if there was anything I hated as much as religion, it was hula-hooping.

I hated hula-hooping with an ugly, inordinate, smoldering contempt. I hated it because I—perhaps like you—*just could not do it*. I didn't know how. And I didn't know how to learn. And I didn't want to. And I didn't care. Like, in any way, at all.

Until, you know—until there was this hot guy.

I.

June, 2005

I feel dead. I would rather be dead. If it weren't for my precious black-brown pit mix, Vincent, I would have no reason to want to be alive. I am out walking him in the midday heat, which is the only thing I ever feel capable of doing apart from going to work, taking showers, chain-smoking cigarettes, and getting wasted on pale ale.

This is not a reflection of reality. This is just how I *feel*. I have a great home, many great friends, and a great job as a mitigation investigator in death-penalty appeals cases. I spend a lot of time driving to weird townships all over the state and interviewing people, which is something I excel at. I excel at it because I am truly interested in every story every person tells me. And they can feel it; they can tell I really want to know, to understand their experiences. So they always tell me a lot.

What I don't have…any longer…is a boyfriend. He dumped me, utterly without ceremony, exactly six months ago. I had just returned from a weekend trip to D.C. He came out to the driveway to meet me when I pulled in. "Aww, he really must have missed me!" I thought gooily, jumping out of the car to hug his tall, lank frame. On the very short trip between the car and the front door, he spun around suddenly to face me and blurted: "I'm moving out!" I realized later he had had to tell me before I got in the house and saw the black line of all his packed suitcases, waiting just inside the front door.

Ever since then, I have been caught in a Groundhog Day warp, living and reliving and reliving the same day. I wake late, my throat thick with mucus from having chain-smoked the night before. Flooded with a ferocious disgust for myself, the thoughts begin to swarm in. *He's gone. He left me. Why did he leave me? How could he leave me? He loved me. I know he loved me. He loves me. I know he loves me. He was just here on Friday!* The disgust thickens into nausea as I pick up my crappy, work-issue Nokia phone and note—with horror—how many calls and texts there are from the night before. All from me to him. He hasn't answered a single one.

9:06 p.m.: *What r u up to tonight?*
10:15 p.m.: *I'm home if u want to come over*
10:48 p.m.: *Vincent says hi*
11:24 p.m.: Outgoing Call
12:08 a.m.: Outgoing Call
12:28 a.m.: *Why won't you answer me?*
1:04 a.m.: *Please just answer me*
1:53 a.m.: *Please...*

Every two or three weeks, he will relent, and spend a night with me. In the morning light, his face looks like a carved wooden mask. He feels nothing. *Why??!!!?* In my heart there is an unquellable, panicked rage that makes no sense. *HOW?!?!??* How did this happen??!! *He was here, we lived together, we have a dog! Why did he leave? Who is he seeing?* The nights when I call and call, I imagine his phone buzzing on the nightstand, over and over and over again. Her (**who????**) asking, "Is everything okay?" My guts clench. The fucking humiliation. The pointless fury, fists swinging into empty air. Him picking up the phone, the garish blue light cupping his face in the dark. The tight look of exasperation as he clicks the ringer to "off" and sets the phone, face down, on the floor. "Don't worry. It's nothing."

I am nothing
I am no one
I do not exist

This lunatic shitshow is, sadly, not new to me. This is actually my third post-breakup meltdown. The last two times, the unbearable feelings eventually just faded out. Each time, it took about a year and a half. I'm only six months in this time. And I have a shrink—a smart one, finally. Yet, this time it seems somehow worse. I seem to have less self-control. The minute I leave work, I buy a six-pack. I smoke steadily while sitting on my porch consuming beer. I call friends. They listen to me tremulously recount the latest installment about the ex. They allow me to cry. It's only been six months. They remember the last two times. They are hoping my agonized mania will wear off, like it did before. But it shows no sign of abating.

My two obligations—my job and my dog—keep me from degenerating entirely into an apparition of nothingness. Otherwise I might never leave my porch, where I sit and smoke and drink and brood on my pain. *Why can't I feel better? Why can't I feel different? What did I do wrong? Why did he leave me? He loved me. There's something wrong with me. Why do I care? Why can't I be with him? If I could just be with him. If he would just let me. I can calm down. I'm calm! I didn't do anything wrong! Why did he leave me?* The questions flit around ceaselessly. They never land. They just buzz and shiver and press against my awareness, demanding my attention. I must *understand*. I must understand how this has happened. But as days and weeks and months go by, still I understand nothing.

Vincent pulls eagerly on his stretchy red leash. He's ecstatic to finally be out walking. The tips of his brownblack ears bob merrily as he prances forth. This tiny motion is the one thing I currently feel able to live for.

Bright needles of pain pierce me from behind my forehead. I haven't had coffee yet. I'm unable to make coffee at home—unless I'm drunk, taking a shower, or asleep, I can't bear to be in the house alone for more than a few minutes.

We are heading to the co-op, a community grocery store that serves as the town's de facto piazza. Everyone in town seems to stop by the co-op at least once a day. It's a hippie haven in the South, where you can find fresh-ground almond butter, organic apples, textured vegetable protein, nutritional yeast. There's also a café with a salad and hot bar. In front of the co-op is a large mulchy yard festooned with green picnic tables. A couple of times a week, from early spring to late summer, bands will set up and play on the lawn, and half the town shows up. Parents spread Indian-print blankets over the mulch and drink wine from paper cups, passing cut-up cheese and grapes to their pleasantly rumpled children, who dart through the crowd and raise clouds of dust with their unrestrained dancing. No band today—just the weekday lunch crowd. I'm sure some friends of mine are sitting amongst them. I make a plan to tie Vincent to a side table and duck inside without seeing anyone. But something catches my eye.

There's someone dancing, alone, in the middle of the lawn. It's a guy. A rangy, dark-haired guy. He just seems to be...dancing, all by himself, with no music, in the middle of the dusty clearing. *How weird is that.* I realize with a start that I recognize him; he's been coming here every day for breakfast for the last few weeks. And he is...I now notice...really... kinda hot. He looks like an early version of Robert Downey Jr: olive skin, straight dark hair, sharp jawline. I have speculated that he's visiting from L.A.; he doesn't look or act like a local guy. He wears mirrored shades and tight-fitting hats and is always talking on a cell phone. I've imagined him as a young cutting-edge entrepreneur with business deals simmering everywhere. But...why...is he out here...dancing?

Somehow, I can't pull my eyes from him. He's *turning,* like a Sufi dervish, around and around and around. His movements are unexpectably graceful and beautiful; he seems to be in some kind of trance. That's when I notice that around him, there is suspended a shape—a black, curving, unending line...a circle. He turns with it; he seems to follow it. He pushes it gently with his body, turning with it through space...with his forearm he lifts it up, into the air, for a single rotation...then—with effortless grace—he sets it back down onto his body. I can't stop staring at him. I mean, what the hell...? He's, like, dancing with this, this... THING, it seems so odd...I can't move, I'm staring at him, at the shape around him, the black line that keeps on moving, rotating, revolving... and all at once I realize that this guy, this cute-as-hell, totally too-cool-looking guy, whirling all by himself in the middle of this public space, he is...the guy is...oh my *god*...he's actually...*hula-hooping!*

6

And for the first time in six grim and long months, my heart and mind heave themselves up out of the dark and terminal cave of loss, and fly like birds toward the seeable truth that is beauty.

II.

Current

"We dance around in a ring and suppose
But the Secret sits in the middle and knows."

— ROBERT FROST

Once the hoop is in flight—once the Point is rotating around and around and around some part (usually the waist) of a living, thinking, moving human body—the hoop might be described, by certain old-school hoopers, as having a "Current."

What the hoop's Current communicates is Flow: the inescapable fact that a hoop in motion is different from a hoop that is resting against the wall. A hoop in motion has an axis: an irreducible center line running vertically through the body, around which the hoop organizes its rotation. This line is purely imaginary: it is something that is felt—*sensed*—by the innate intelligence of the body. It cannot be observed or measured by the instruments we might use to measure particles or valences or thermodynamics or gravity or any thing we may assert to be materially "real."

But can you assert that the center of a rotating hoop does not exist?

If a rotating hoop had no center, it could not be in a state of rotation.

** (Pause for reminder that asserting anything using a hula-hoop as your central metaphor is an act so absurd that no word yet exists to describe it.)

III.

September, 1973

I am three years old. I'm sitting in our upstairs hallway, on the brown shag carpet, leaning heavily against my brother's closed bedroom door. I am alone, except for my Raggedy Ann doll, who snuggles in the crook of my arm. There is a painful longing in my chest—it pushes pushes pushes against the bedroom door, but like my small hands, it is not enough to get to my mother, to the sound of her voice, murmuring low just on the other side of this impossibly tall white divide. I have never before been disallowed contact with her.

I hear my brother, his proud voice carrying easily through the thick wood. Hot rage bolts through me. He has just started first grade, and they have begun to learn to read. Every day, now, when he comes home from school, he gets to have our mother all to himself for an hour while he practices reading. The unfairness of this roils my insides with a horrible specificity. *He can...I can't.* The thought is unbearable. It's not *fair* that he gets to be alone with her while I have to sit out here in the hall! *IT'S! NOT! FAIR!* The wrongness makes me feel like my chest will split open. But—I know that there is nothing I can do. It has been decided. He is learning to read and that is more important than me. I have to sit alone with Raggedy Ann while he cuddles with Mom in the safety of his own room, where I am never, ever allowed to go. I sit, waiting.

My brother's voice doesn't sound like it does when he is talking. He pauses heavily between every word or two. "Sam…is…a boy. Sam…ll-likes…the dog." Excited, he sucks the excess saliva from his teeth with a quick *cchhh* sound. "Sam…thh…thh…throwwws…the ball…to the…dog." I know that they are both looking down at the big book with the purple and green stripe on the cover, and that is the special thing that makes my brother's voice sound different and holds the power to pull my mother entirely away from me. "The dog…runs. Sam runs…wi…wi…with…him." I concentrate, so as not to be left out entirely. I focus my entire being on the words my brother is speaking. I will make it so that I cannot be shut out anymore. "Sal-ly runs…too."

Later, after the door is finally opened and my mother is returned to me, I sneak back upstairs. My brother is outside, playing Kick the Can with our neighbors Danny and David. He won't come back in until dark. My mother is downstairs in the kitchen, listening to the radio and making stew. The herby stew smell follows me up the twisty back staircase lined with a fuzzy red carpet my mother hates. The fuzzy red carpet is my very favorite thing about this house, but my mother says it's "tacky." I think she means "full of tacks" so I am always very careful when I walk up and down them. I get to my brother's bedroom door, listening intently as I push it open, making no sound as I walk in.

The white-purple-green book sits on the blue table between his twin beds. I pull it over onto the nearest bed—the hard one he never sleeps in—and slide it squarely in front of me so I can open it. I pull open the cover, glancing up every few seconds to look out my brother's bedroom door. My heart is thumping. If he finds me in his room, he will punch me in the face. That is a certainty.

I look down at the first page and see a pale painting of a boy with black hair and a light blue shirt standing on a sidewalk, with a straight line of squiggly-straight words written beneath. I know, from watching *Sesame Street* and *The Electric Company* on TV every day, that the first big curvy snake-shaped letter makes a snake-like sound: "*sssssssss.*" As I, very quietly, say the *sssss* sound, looking at the first word, I remember the name I heard my brother say, *Sam*. And I realize that must be what I am looking at. "Ssssssaaaammm," I whisper to myself, slowly. And then I see—the very next word *ends* with the ssssame sssound-- "*Sssssam...i-i-i-issssss*," and I realize that the tiny tiny word next to Sam must be *is*, because I remember: *Sam is a boy*. I whisper the two words almost silently *(don't make a ssssound)* to myself: "Sssssaaamm issss... Sssaamm isss...Ssaam iss..." until I know that I know them. And I do.

For the next few weeks, I slip into my brother's room every chance I get, heart hammering, looking at the pages, looking at the pictures, looking for letters I recognize from *Sesame Street* and *Electric Company*, and matching them all to the words and sentences I remember hearing. "Mmmm...mmmm...mmmakesssss...Ssssssam mmmakes-ss...hiiissss...b-b-beddd. Sssam mmakess hiss bed." Every day it makes more sense. I recognize three words, five, ten, thirty. "Sam g-g-goes to the ssstore." I know what a store is. "Sam and hisss mmmommy carrrry the b-b-bags." I have seen all the letters on TV. All I have to do is look at a letter, remember its sound from TV, and connect it to the words I have memorized while leaning unhappily against the closed door, waiting for my hour of exile to be over. Soon I know all the words in the book—or, most of them. I can read all the words. I can read.

One morning I am alone with Mom in the kitchen. She is wearing her long blue slippy robe I like. I like to stay close to her in the kitchen, and smell her coffee. Sometimes she will let me have a tiny, tiny sip. Her coffee cup—the brown one, with silvery specks like snowflakes and stripes up the side—sits at her place at the table beside the newspaper my mother and father read every day. I climb up on her chair, looking down at the newspaper, trying to make out the big, bold headlines. Mom stands at the sink doing dishes while I pore over the paper, quietly.

"What are you doing, Annie?" Mom asks, a smile in her voice.

"Reading," I say, affecting a casual tone, as if I do this all the time. I'm ready to get MY daily hour alone with her.

"You haven't learned to read yet, honey," she says mildly.

"I can too!" I say loudly. It hasn't occurred to me that she wouldn't *believe* me. "*I can!*" I shout for emphasis. (*He can...I can.*)

"You can read that?" says Mom, in a way that tells me she still doesn't believe me.

"Yes," I say defensively, even though I have seen several words that I don't recognize. I look down at one big headline I recognize most of and start to read it out loud: "F...fi...firrssst...b...bl...black...mmay..or...ell-lec...ted...in At...lllan...ta." I look up at her triumphantly.

"Annie!" she breathes, sweeping over to me in one step, delight singing in her voice. "How did you learn that?"

I hesitate, realizing that if I reveal my sneaky scheme, it could get back to my brother, and I might get punched in the face. "I just...did," I say, realizing instantly that this doesn't explain enough. Already, I have a piercing terror of lying. *Sneaking* is okay, but *lying*—using words to hide the truth—isn't. Quickly, I add, "I listened to you and Greg, when he was reading, through the door," thinking this will be enough for her. It is.

"Your daddy will be *so proud!*" She's looking at me, smiling a very special smile I haven't seen on her face before. Her hand is around my shoulder, like a friend.

I look for a few more big headline words I can read: "Nnno...bel...pee...ack."

"Peace," my mother says. "It says, 'peace.'" She is beaming at me.

"Pr...preee...prize...gi...vven...to...Hen...Hen...Hen...er..."

"Henry," my mom says.

"Kissss...kissss..." unable to finish the long name, I look up at Mom.

"Kissinger," she finishes, her voice lifted with pride. I grin back at her, my heart swelling. I have won my own special status with Mom. It no longer matters if I get the hour of solo reading time—I have learned to read *all by myself.*

I turn back to the paper. I see more and more words on it that I know. I'm ready to know all of them, to read *all* of them. My feet feel firm on the seat of the cane chair. I can read. I feel power rush through my entire body as my small hands grab hold of the reins of the world. Now, there's nothing anyone can know that I can't. I can understand anything now; I can understand everything.

IV.

Flow

Just remain in the center; watching.
And then forget that you are there.

- Lao Tzu

When a hooper feels the Point to the extent that she successfully establishes a Current, and the fullness of her attention—body, mind, and spirit—is focused, wholly and unerringly, towards its sustenance, she may be said to be in Flow.

The Flow state, as a phenomenon, has been most thoroughly researched and explicated by a Hungarian psychologist with the famously unpronounceable name of Mihály Csíkszentmihályi, who built his legendary career studying the elusive human mood we call "happiness." He has defined the Flow state as a state of "effortless attention." In the Flow state, one is "completely involved in an activity for its own sake. The ego falls away. Time flies. Every action, movement, and thought follows inevitably from the previous one, like playing jazz."

In Taoism, there is a concept known as *wu wei,* which can be understood to mean "effortless action." The image most often associated with this quality is flowing water. To a Taoist, this quality of flow stands above all qualities and properties of the universe we know ourselves to be experiencing in this moment. The word "tao" does not translate to mean "God," but rather "way" or "path." For a Taoist, the universe is not something to be mastered, overcome, or transcended, but rather, something to be *moved with.* The embodied practices—Qi Gong, T'ai Chi—teach us not how to think or what to believe, but rather how to feel and flow with Way.

In Western religious traditions, thinking is prized above feeling: it is more important to have the right *ideas* about God, and to evaluate your behavior according to these ideas. God is understood as a separate, evaluative, punitive presence who metes out rewards or punishments based on the correctness of one's beliefs and—in some cases—actions. By contrast, the Tao is a context so simultaneously vast and omnipresent that it may only be approached through metaphor, or through embodied practice—i.e., indirect methods of knowing, which require a measure of surrender.

If you have lost a loved one—an immediate family member, perhaps—then you might be familiar with those things toward which one may only cultivate a relationship of surrender.

V.

I am standing in my peach-carpeted bedroom, carefully combing my damp, shoulder-length hair. The floor is dotted with large brown packing boxes, open at the top like cubist flowers. In two weeks, I will be leaving home to fly up to New York City, where I will begin my studies at a Seven Sisters school. This achievement is the culmination of all the relentless efforts of the last four years.

Throughout high school, I have had almost no social life. The tiny all-girl academy I just graduated from has filled up almost every available hour with classes, study halls, after-school activities, daily homework, and—of course—rampant silliness with my friends. I have not missed—one bit—having boys in school. Rather, their disappearance from my daily life has been an unimaginable relief. At the end of my first week of ninth grade at the girls' school—a parentally-forced matriculation I had dreaded for months—I sat, stunned, on my mother's porch, swinging absently in the wooden porch swing, clutching my brand-new school bookbag—fat with all my new textbooks—to my chest like a precious infant. *I have never been so happy*, I sat repeating to myself for long, dazed minutes. *I've just never been this happy.*

With boys gone, I have been free to immerse myself in the culture of the girls' school, which is predicated upon the character and excellence of its students. At my coed public middle school, the culture demanded underachievement: you did all your homework and made good grades, *bam!* You were an automatic loser. The most popular students were those who demonstrated their contempt for authority by sneaking smokes, getting sent out in the hall, grabbing other kids' asses, and shouting swear words as loudly as possible. At the girls' school, this script is squarely flipped—the most admired and popular girls are those who embody the cardinal virtues: the nicest, best-behaved, smartest, and most well-rounded students among us are also the most well-liked and powerful. Hence, my book-nerdiness—a terrible liability in middle school—has been transformed into one of my best assets.

Though I, like all the other girls at school, have enjoyed only the barest minimum of a social life these past four years, I have found certain appropriate, good-girl outlets. A main outlet for me has been the weekly meeting of Young Life, an interdenominational Christian youth group that meets in a rec hall behind the Methodist church every Wednesday. I started going my freshman year, riding along with my brother—a senior—who would go every week to play guitar for the group singalongs that inaugurate every meeting.

The singalongs begin as boisterous affairs, everyone shouting at the top of our voices to songs we all know by heart: Beatles, Creedence, Commodores. Gradually, the songs shade over into church camp clap-and-sings:

IIIIIII've got PEACE
Like a river, I've got PEACE
Like a river, I've got PEACE
Like a river, in my soouuuuull
(in my sooouuuulll)

The songs invariably devolve into emotional ballads: Michael W. Smith, Amy Grant, James Taylor's "You've Got a Friend." By the end of the singalong, you often hear the sound of tears being snuffled back; some kids throw an arm around their neighbor, who might be weeping quietly.

After we sing, one of the good-looking, charismatic youth leaders will stand and give a short talk about their relationship with Jesus. My favorite one is Ty, the main leader. His blazing blue eyes pierce you with sincerity. And his talks are always the best. People *always* cry when he speaks. After the youth leader witnesses, they pick a high school student (often a cute upperclassman) to speak last, to share a story of his or her walk with Christ. I've never stood up to witness—it's not my style.

Though I love the warm closeness and camaraderie of the YL meetings and admire the cool youth leaders boundlessly, I have been raised to observe faith as an intensely personal matter. My favorite Bible verse—which I have bookmarked and underlined and reread frequently—is Matthew 6:6: "But when you pray, go into your room, close the door, and pray to your Father, who is unseen. Then your Father, who sees what is done in secret, will reward you." I've never followed the YL directive to (politely and respectfully) proselytize—it just doesn't feel right to me. I only read my Bible by myself, in the privacy of my own room; I only pray silently, for God alone to hear. My parents never ask me what God I believe in, or why. In my family, one's spiritual walk is understood to be one's own private business.

I haven't always felt so closely aligned with Christ's message. When I was very small, our entire family attended the stereotypically dull Presbyterian church: no shouting, no hugging, no clapping, and most definitely no spontaneous witnessing. Services in the massive, quiet sanctuary were carefully orchestrated: the minister swept in, long robes fluttering, as the music of an immense organ resounded off the arched ceiling, announcing his arrival. A large choir carried most of the uninspiring hymns—people in the congregation sang so mildly it was difficult to hear even the person right next to you. We stood and sat, recited prayers, and listened to the minister's long, boring sermon. In the pauses between, no one ever made a sound.

But when I was seven years old, my parents abruptly announced they were divorcing, and all of the sudden my father started attending another church…a very, very different church. It was called Unitarian Universalist. We never had to dress up (you could wear jeans! Shorts!) and no one ever seemed to mention God at all. If we spent Saturday night with Daddy—which we often did—we would go with him on Sunday morning to the UU. Other Sundays, we would go to the Presbyterian church with

Mom. My brother and I preferred the UU—we liked not having to dress up and being free to roam around and play with the other kids while the adults sat in the polygonal sanctuary, listening not to a sermon given by a minister, but to a serious talk about institutional racism or political upheaval in Nicaragua, delivered by a visiting scholar or activist. There were no hymns—there were not even hymnals. No Sunday school—we kids were free to play on the playground, create art projects, or hang out with the adults who were babysitting the littlest kids. I had a hard time understanding what Unitarians actually *believed*.

However, after a few years of random attendance at the UU, one morning I was playing with a group of kids on the swing set. One suddenly asked out loud what we, as Unitarians, believed. After a short group attempt at establishing a credo, one of the older boys shouted, "Hang on a minute, y'all!" and ran off to the church vestibule. He came running back, panting and holding out a trifold from the greeting table. "Here's what we believe," he said. "Right here!" He opened the pamphlet to show a large, hand-drawn circle. Within the circle were all the symbols of the world's major religions: the Star of David, the Cross, the Yin/Yang, the Star and Crescent, the Aum, the Buddhist Wheel. Above it was printed: "The Circle of Oneness." I felt immediately certain that this radical inclusivity was exactly equivalent to the teachings of Jesus, who would turn away no one. And for a long time afterward, I wasn't really bothered by the split personality of my religious education.

But since I started attending Young Life meetings, it *has* begun to bother me that my father seems to have roundly rejected the teachings and authority of Christ. I haven't understood this, and tried one day to talk to him about it. We were sitting in the car, in the driveway at Mom's house. He was dropping me off. I stammered out (why did I feel *embarrassed?*) my question: Did he believe in God?

"Annie," he said, focusing his clear blue eyes on the rearview mirror, in which the sun was slowly sinking. His Eastern North Carolina accent is lilting and musical, and his expressive and precise way of speaking makes every sentence into a kind of song. "I believe in...*some* kind of...higher power." He paused, looking me in the eye. My father always speaks to me as to any other adult. "I'm not sure, however, that we can know exactly what that power is."

"But…" I countered, confused by his answer. A *higher power* might refer to some kind of God, which seems…right, I guess. But what about Jesus? To me, it is Jesus that is important. Jesus, after all, is God on Earth. "Do you…believe in…" (my face getting hot with the effort of speaking such unutterable things) "Do you believe that Jesus was…the Son of God?"

"I believe…" he began, the long e's gliding sweetly against his sharp consonants. "I believe that Jesus was—a great *teacher,* and did a great deal to bring *peace* to the world." He looked up again at the setting sun in the rearview. "But there are certain…beliefs, in Christianity that are too…too…" and here he searched, an uncharacteristically long time, for exactly the right word: "—*mystical* for me."

My face burned as if I had been slapped. *Mystical???* I felt my throat close around this horrible insult. My father just equated the holy person of Jesus Christ with the new age frippery of Tarot readings and runic divination. How could he say such a thing!? I reacted with my standard anger default: slipping irretrievably into a safe and unreachable silence. And I have kept silent about this topic ever since.

But my father and I are on the exact same page when it comes to the advancement of my education. Even though I researched my potential college choices on my own—reading a 500-page college guide from cover to cover, taking copious notes and creating my own ranking system based on student reviews of each English department—he and Mom have both taken me on extensive trips to visit and narrow down my list of faves. While both my parents are thrilled that I will be attending a great school in a glorious city, I can tell it's my dad who has been made happiest by my choice. Mom will miss me around the house, possibly wishing deep down that I would go somewhere closer to home—though she would never, ever, ever say so. But it is my father who has most specifically envisioned this ivy-encrusted future for me. When I called Daddy at the office to tell him I had gotten the letter, with its august blue seal, saying that yes, in fact, I was invited to join the

Class of '92 in the world's greatest city, I could hear the special joy in his musical voice. "Of *course* you did!" he shouted. "Of *course* you did!"

* * *

The phone brrrrrrings, interrupting my end-of-summer reverie. I wonder if it's my friend Lisle...in a few minutes, I'm driving to her house to pick her up, and we're going to the pool. We've been working as counselors at a YMCA camp all summer, so this will be one of our summer's only pool trips. I need to try and grab a decent tan before moving up to New York.

But it must not be her, because Mom doesn't call for me. I wonder if I'm about to be late. I shoot a glance at the teal-blue digital clockface on my bedside table: 3:10 p.m. I have a few more minutes before I have to leave. Quickly, I finish the careful parting of my hair and turn to my wardrobe, folding things into my canvas shoulder bag. *Blue bikini...Hawaiian Tropic...towel...soccer shorts...t-shirt...*

"Ann!" My mother's voice issues sharply from downstairs.

"What is it?" I yell back, irked but also aware that she is using my proper name, which has to mean something serious. I hope I haven't left the stove on, or the keys in the car.

"Come out here!" she shouts, her South Carolina accent blasting forth along with her heightened stress. *Ay-unn! Cuhm aayyout heeyer!* I wish my brother was here to laugh with me, silently. Making fun of our parents is our main bonding activity. Though my eyes roll the teeniest bit, I zap obediently out into the hallway and over to the balustrade, where I can look down at her, standing in the foyer. Her face looks pale and strangely expressionless.

"What's up?" I chirp, already angling to minimize what is probably a fabricated urgency. Maybe the dog has wandered down to the boarding house again—I can run and get her before I leave.

"Your Daddy just called," she says. "He needs you to come over there *right now*. He needs to talk to you."

Talk to me?!?! I bristle at the rare direct command. I'm about to pick up *Lisle*. We're going to the *pool*. I'm supposed to be over there in 15 minutes! Why does he have to talk to me *right now?!* Annoyance spikes my tone as I holler down to the ground floor: "Why?!"

"There's something…wrong"—and here she waves her hand in a wide, single motion, indicating an unconsidered magnitude— "with his *brain.*"

Her voice wavers as it passes over that last word. I hear what she has said. I understand the meaning of the words she has used. But I know— there can't possibly be anything wrong with my father's brain. My father is the smartest person any of us knows; he never forgets a name or misses a question on *Jeopardy!,* and his flourishing law practice depends on the reliable accuracy and precision of his ever-active mind. On every level, he's always moving just a little bit faster than other people. People jog just to keep up with him walking, everyone remembers him, everyone reaches out for a handshake or hug as he passes by tables in a restaurant. He's often asked when he will finally run for mayor. My father's brain is the engine that has built the foundation of our entire lives. It is simply not possible that something could be wrong with it.

Despite my instinctive doubt, however—I know I need to get over to my dad's house, pronto. Whenever he does issue one of his infre- quent commands, my brother and I hop to, right away. To oppose him would be unthinkable.

In five minutes, I am pulling up in the little parking area behind my dad's renovated three-story Victorian, less than a mile from Mom's. The top two floors are divided into apartments; Daddy lives on the ground floor. His back door is never locked.

Though normally I would just walk in, I find myself unable to. I stand at the back door, peering through the wavy glass panels. My father is clear-minded and decisive; he is never at a loss as to what to do. Finally, I knock, quietly. *Tok..tok tok…*

Instantly he appears, looking powerfully healthy in his weekend out- fit (though it is not the weekend): bright pink polo shirt, khaki shorts, and an unflattering and incongruous pair of lumpy brown Birkenstock sandals—the favorite and regular target of my brother's and my ridicule. My father opens the door and without a word enfolds me into one of his strong, steady hugs, which for a moment holds the world absolutely still.

For a moment, I can stop thinking, and relax into the certainty that everything will, in fact, be okay. He will not allow it to be otherwise.

He motions me into his room; we sit on the edge of his bed, facing one another. This is where, before my brother left for college, the three of us would snuggle in a pile to watch the heavy old TV that sinks down into the front edge of the black leather ottoman it is perched on. I haven't continued this tradition with my father—I have been too busy with my hours of homework and extracurriculars to waste time watching TV. The bulky television always looks like any second it will fall face-first onto the ivory rug of my father's bedroom. But it doesn't fall.

Characteristically, my father cuts straight to the point. "Annie," he begins, looking me precisely in the eye, "there is something wrong with my brain." He uses the same disinterested, descriptive tone he would use to explain the three branches of government, or best practices when driving a car. As always, he clearly enunciates every syllable. "We do not know yet what it is. We will find out tomorrow morning, when I have a biopsy. However, there are three possibilities."

He holds one palm face up and the other perpendicular, like a knife. When he speaks again, he slices his upper hand, point by point, down into his flat palm. "It could be an abscess, which would be the least serious situation; it could be a benign tumor, which would mean I might have to have surgery; or it could be a malignant tumor, which would be the most serious possibility." I do not take my eyes from him as he speaks, forcing myself to concentrate on the meaning of his words—words I have never heard him say before. *Biopsy...abscess...benign...malignant.* "Whatever the case may be," he continues briskly, "Whatever the case may be, whatever we find out tomorrow, I want you to understand that in two weeks, you *will* be leaving for school as scheduled." His open knife-hand points right at me now. "You will not stay here, you will not delay your enrollment, you will not interrupt your education for any reason. Is that clear."

I do not move my eyes from his as a nauseating wave breaks over me: it has not even crossed my mind to stay here. It has not occurred to me even for one moment to give up my new life in New York, to remain here with my father and help him through whatever struggle he might be facing. The ungodly depth of my selfishness jerks the breath from my body. I cannot move. I do not dare make any motion, anything that might betray the inhuman scope of my unnatural self-obsession. I cannot allow him to see the perverse and revolting truth that has just fallen on me from an empty sky: I do not love him.

He is looking at me, expecting the assent he knows I will deliver. I have to deliver it. "Yes sir," I say quickly, keeping my eyes fixed on his. Of course I am leaving. Of course I am going to New York. Of course I am starting school. Of course I am not looking back. This has been the plan—this has always been the plan. But never attended by this awful cold emptiness, this freakish absence of love, this sickening narcissism. My insides sink down, down…I am one of the wrong kind of people. I am unable to feel; I am unable to love.

"Okay. Good," he says, the lines around his eyes relaxing the tiniest bit. In a panic to cover over the terrifying revelation of my inhumanity, I try to make a joke: "Hey, you kinda sss-ssscared me—" but my voice squeaks up into nothingness as weirdly cold tears begin to slip from my eyes. My father clasps me in another strong hug which does nothing to quell the dread of my grotesque self-absorption. I can't even cry right—I'm not sobbing, just leaking curiously unwarm tears onto his shoulder. This isn't real.

After a moment, he releases me and jumps up, offering his hand. He doesn't have any more time to comfort me. His eyes are already pointed ahead, to the next task. I am to leave the gloomy interior of this old Victorian and head out into the persistent sunshine where I will meet my friends at the pool. He will dash to the office to meet up with two of his closest friends who will help him deal with whatever paperwork needs to be dealt with—just in case. Just in case he can't make it back to the office for a while. He will probably be awake all night, taking care of everything that needs to be taken care of before his appointment in the morning. But I, of course, don't think of this. I'm flooded with guilt and relief to be liberated from this grim interlude, my thoughts rushing back to the preexisting day. I wonder if any of the guys from Lisle's high school will show up at the pool.

He walks me to the back door, giving me one more of his sturdy hugs. As we say goodbye, we exchange our traditional series of "butter-fly," "Eskimo," and "littlest" kisses. "I love you," he says, as always, in his musical way. And before I turn away and walk out again into the searing-ly bright sunlight, I—as always—say it back to him.

VI.

Rhythm

Meet it, and you do not see its beginning.
Follow it, and you do not see its end.
Stay with the ancient Way
in order to master what is present.

—LAO TZU

How did you decide what it is that you believe?

When I was 18, I wasn't aware of having made any decisions about my beliefs. I thought I just knew what was right. I *felt* my rightness, deep down inside. My beliefs about God, about our world, about what could be considered to be real, felt unshakeable—until the world around me began itself to shake.

When we play, when we dance, when we *flow*, we change our relationship to time. We move out of linear time—that narrative, "beginning-middle-end" time that defines our day-to-day lives and identities—and into the cyclical time that governs the perceptible universe: an endlessly self-renewing revolution of forms and patterns whose relationships to one another depend on rhythm.

Our own intrinsic sense of *rhythm* is what we discover when we successfully get the hoop to revolve around our waist. We all share this innate sense of rhythm...yes! Even you who insist that you "can't dance"! In fact, I already know that you can both hula-hoop AND dance. And if you try to argue with me on this point, I shall simply point out that you taught yourself how to walk before you could possibly begin to understand what walking even was.

You taught yourself how to walk because your infant body was built to understand and to follow *rhythm*. You taught yourself how to walk by *feeling* that rhythm—an equal shift of your body weight from side to side—because you certainly couldn't talk yet. Or, even if you could already say "Mama" or "baby," you could not—at age one—comprehend the complex dynamics involved in propelling a human body across a surface while fully at the mercy of gravity. You had an intrinsic, inborn sense of *rhythm*—the same wisdom we tap into when we learn how to hula-hoop.

Seriously, though.

VII.

I once asked a bird, "How is it that you fly
in this gravity of darkness?"

She responded, "Love lifts me."

— HAFIZ

June, 2005

I'm sitting at one of the green picnic tables outside the co-op, having lunch
with my best guy friend, Kimowan. He's a professor of art at the university.
We've been friends since the moment we were introduced at a community
art show four years ago. His three pieces were the standouts of the show—
conceived as a creative exploration of a years-abandoned textile mill in a
neighboring county, each artist using some of the everyday objects left behind in the mill for unique installation pieces. I noticed I kept getting stuck
in front of works by "Kimowan McLain," unable to stop admiring all that
was happening with so little material. My favorite piece was the one placed
last in the show. By then I knew that this Kimowan, whoever he or she may
be, was one of the best artists I would ever meet in person.

The finale piece consisted of few elements. On a round black table,
almost chest-height, lay a feathery gray dead moth. From high up in the
old beams, a single tracklight encircled the moth. And high above the

moth, suspended from the beams by an impossibly light, almost invisible string (I learned later it was strands of his long black hair, tied end-to-end), floated the curled, banded body of a dead wasp. The wasp-husk shifted with every little puff of air, so that its sharp, black shadow over the dead moth hovered and trembled with life. Death and its shadow, entwined in beautiful simplicity. Entwined in dance.

Our friendship is automatic, self-evident, easy. Often, we just can't stop talking—we'll sit out here, yammering steadily about Cy Twombly, the internet, Beyoncé, powwow ritual, William Eggleston, Jung, Buddhism, Canadian soft rock, Werner Herzog, Outkast, and/or color theory, until we notice that the sun has moved perilously close to the treeline, and an entirely different sea of faces surrounds us. "I gotta get back to the studio," Kimo (an American riff on his Canadian nickname, "Kim") will say, unbending himself with quick grace and beelining around the corner to his old white Honda four-door. He'll stay there til late, maybe enjoy a smoke and a nighttime chat with one of his art pals—Jeff, or Pat Day.

It being summer, Kimo doesn't have any classes or students to prepare for, so we are having a leisurely extended meal; which is to say, we have been here since breakfast and ended up just barreling on through lunch, adding to our coffee cups and plates as needed. My job as a mitigation investigator, driving around to strange and unprosperous towns all over the state, keeps my workdays individually long but somewhat widely spaced.

"How are ya, sweetie?" Kimo, like all my closest crew, knows about my self-imposed breakup *agon*.

"Ehhh…" I was born only 75 miles from here, but have taken on shades of my friend's Canadianness—as he has adopted "y'all" and "haaay."

"Ya gotta get back out there! Start datin' some dudes!"

"How could I possibly choose between college kids and sad, desperate alcoholics?"

"Aw, you *know* there are some decent guys here still, Annie."

"I'm too pathetic right now. It's affected my eyesight."

"That guy over there looks interesting…" He indicates a light-eyed, bushy-browed Teutonic hulk, devouring a mound of hot bar food. This is the kind of guy only other guys think women are into.

"Bssshhhhhh!…" I frown. I'm being a child. But I cannot abide guys with blond eyelashes.

Kimo doesn't actually like having to give me pep talks. He prefers to follow the strange, ranging curve of pure mind, buddy-swimming in and out of the observational matrix. But he's trying really, really hard, just for my sake. He hates to see me so pained. Our romantic potential was annihilated from the outset by his summer romance a couple years back with one of my closest girlfriends. The three of us were so often together and ridiculous, and their breakup so long and mutually excruciating, that by the time they finally achieved separation he was my forever bfam. The world's best kind of relationship.

"Hey, Baxter!" Kimo shouts, looking past me and raising his arm. "Baxter!" he says, smiling hugely.

I turn my head to see *the hoop guy*. He is walking towards us, carrying a large coffee and a little tower of food. I have forgotten all about him. I am stunned. What am I wearing?! DEAR GOD!

"Hey there," Baxter The Hoop Guy says, smiling cutely down at our table.

"Hey, man!" I have never seen Kimo so excited to see somebody. He slaps his hand into Baxter's open palm and pulls him in for a man-hug. "Sit down and have lunch with us!"

"Thanks, Kimo, man," Baxter says and sits down across from me. He pronounces Kimo's name more like "Kimmo" (whereas I say "KEE-mo"). Maybe he thinks it sounds more Canadian.

"This is my friend, Annie," Kimo says, indicating me with a flourish of his hand across the table.

"Hi!" I say, extending my hand and a smile far wider than the occasion calls for.

Baxter sets down his lunch, pulls off his iridescent shades, and shakes my hand with a firm warmth. He was brought up right. He sits down across the table. His eyes are dark brown and sweetly parenthesized by smile lines. He's tanned, lithe, and muscular. Heavy eyebrows (always a plus in my book) and an ever-so-slightly large nose in between his wide forehead and angled chin. For lunch, he has bought a seeded roll, a quarter pound of tuna salad, an avocado, and a gargantuan cup of coffee. With a tiny white plastic knife, he begins to cut the roll in half to assemble a sandwich. His DIY meal strikes me as intensely adorable. I concentrate on keeping my smile at a socially acceptable wattage while trying to prevent stray runnels of coffee from dribbling down my chin.

"How's the hoopin?" Kimo asks buoyantly.

"Real good, my friend, real good—" says Baxter, finishing his careful roll-slicing and moving on to the more challenging project of the avocado.

"Baxter does this hoop-dancing, Annie..."—Kimo turns his brightened face to me—"it's just...amazing!" Such praise from my friend, who made his way out of a life of chronic poverty and chaos solely on the strength of his artistic and intellectual gifts, is tough to win.

"I know! I saw you—" I clamp down on the note of lunatic joy in my voice.

"You did?!" Baxter seems genuinely shocked.

"Yeah, the other day! Over there—" I gesture towards the lawn. "It really was...amazing." Can I not think of anything more interesting to say? *Faaaaaaaaahhhhhck! Okay, whatever, Ann, just don't freak out. Do not. Freak. Out.*

"Well thank you," Baxter says, the familiar sweetness of his local accent (*thenk yew*) shooting into my heart like a drug. All I can think to do is smile. Again.

"What you're doin with that hoop, man—" Kimo swivels back to Baxter, "—it's freakin...*awesome*. I mean—wow." Have I ever heard him say *wow*? "Back home we have hoopdancers"—Kimo hails from a tiny Indigenous (he would say *Indian*) reservation (he would say *reserve*) way the hell up in Northern Alberta (*Cold Lake First Nations!* he will say, grinning and throwing the "CL" sign in front of his chest)—"and they use the small hoops, a whole bunch of em, to make shapes. It's a whole different thing. They don't do the one hoop around the body. Each shape has a character, a story—like the eagle, or the owl. But you're really taking it to another place."

"I appreciate that, man. Really."

"You still got that hoop class?"

31

Baxter nods. "For sure. Every Monday."

"Annie, we should go!" Kimo says, turning back to me with an expression of pure delight.

I nod and—of course—smile, riding a sudden, chilly wave of apprehension as it flashes before me: I cannot hula-hoop. Like. At. All. "Totally!" I gush, allowing my excess romantic gaiety to camouflage this new undertow of benign dread.

"We'll come next Monday!" Kimo confirms, sending shock waves through my stomach.

"What if..." I begin. Baxter and Kimo both turn and look at me, waiting. "What if you...I mean..." *Jesus Christ! Just say it!* "What if I can't... actually...hula-hoop? I've never been able to." A sudden horrible memory twists up in my mind: I am five years old, in the yard at our babysitter's house, laboring to get a hula-hoop going around my waist while my brother and the other kids point and laugh, hoops effortlessly whirling around their bodies. My hoop drops to the ground, again, and again, and again, my face burning with humiliation. I speculate to myself: *Maybe I can go to the class, but just not hula-hoop. Maybe I can just sit and watch.*

"Oh, you can," says Baxter, waving off my mounting anxiety. "You just need a big hoop."

"A BIG hoop?" This strikes me as manifestly wrong. How could a bigger hoop be easier? A *small* one should be easier. Kimo also looks confused.

"Totally. Big hoops are much easier than small hoops."

"They ARE?" I say.

"Really?" says Kimo.

"Yes, absolutely. Think of it this way...." Baxter has obviously explained this many times before. "Small hoops, we call them toy hoops, are made for kids. The proportion is correct for a kid's body." He points one finger down and draws circles in the air. "But an adult's body is bigger, not just taller but *wider*. So a bigger hoop,"—and here he widens the circles—"makes a bigger circle. And it goes around more slowly." The instant he completes this short explanation, I realize how utterly sensible and, in fact, self-evident it is. Of *course* big hoops are easier!

"Yeah! I see!" Simple glee rings in my voice.

"Hunh…" Kimo—distracted by being wrong about something—sounds a bit less effusive. In a moment he will adjust, and then proceed as though he knew this fact all along.

Baxter steals a glance at me, and his eyes hold a tiny twinkle. I will…I *will*…go to his hooping class next Monday. And I will—for the first time in my life—hula-hoop. I just feel it.

* * *

The following Monday, Kimo and I climb a carpeted staircase to the second floor of a local movement studio. Powerful rhythms bounce off the maize-colored walls. We walk into a large room with blond laminate flooring where Baxter and several women whirl gracefully inside a multicolored array of hoops. Baxter stands at the far end of the room, swaying inside his lazily revolving black hoop. Tied around his head, fully covering his eyes, is a wide black bandana. What the…?

A couple of people smile and wave us in, pointing to the stack of *big hoops* leaning against one wall. Kimo and I walk over and begin rifling through the different colors and sizes. Hearing the hoops shuffle, Baxter tilts his head back and peers out from beneath his bandana. Seeing us, his face breaks into a big grin.

"Hey, y'all!" he calls, walking over and putting a hand on each of our shoulders. "Have you found some hoops you like?"

"I'm thinkin about this one," says Kimo, holding up a royal blue hoop with a single band of white tape around one segment. It's one of the medium-sized ones, not the biggest. I know him; he doesn't want to start with the easiest size.

"Sure, man, go for it," says Baxter. I can tell he might be thinking that Kimo should start bigger, but knows better than to say so.

"What about this one?" I am holding a big heavy hoop, covered in a stretchy velveteen fabric with a leopard print. I have chosen the only hoop that shows discernible sex appeal.

"That's a nice one," Baxter concurs with a smile and a nod. I smile back with reckless zeal.

Clinging to the memory of my eight years of yoga like an invisible blankie, I watch Baxter carefully as he explains to me and Kimo how to get the hoop started. "First, place both feet wide apart. All right. Now put one foot slightly in front of the other. Okay. Now you've got a good foundation. Just hold the hoop in both hands, and wind it up to one side—" he twists to one side, holding the hoop around his waist, fitting it snugly against his lower back. We follow. "And then *throw* it, straight across your body"—he shoots the hoop to the other side, into rotation—"and start rocking back and forth, back and forth, back and forth…" I watch him carefully for a minute, then launch my big hoop to the right and start rocking like crazy, feeling its mass and momentum swing around me. I rock back and forth on my feet, back and forth, back and forth…and…it…doesn't…fall!

It goes around seven, eight, nine times—*whoosh whoosh whoosh whoosh*—before I feel it start to spiral down. It plonks to the floor, the soft fabric muffling its impact. "I DID IT!" I shout. I am five years old. I look over at Baxter. "IT WORKED!"

"Yeah!" he affirms, grinning adorably.

I start again. Eight, nine, ten, eleven…*plonk*. And again: ten, eleven, twelve, thirteen, fourteen…*plonk*.

I look over at Kimo. Baxter has convinced him to try a bigger hoop. He has a huge, bright orange circle swinging around and around his dramatically forward-leaning torso. His hands are up in a kind of boxer's stance, fists together. I remember he used to box as a teenager. It's the only sport he has ever participated in. Kimo doesn't rock back and forth, but jumps up and down, landing heavily on the floor. His mouth is open, eyes closed. He hops from foot to foot. It's not what Baxter is recommending, but it looks cool. I will later understand that he is using his powwow dance moves inside the hoop. Every skill he has ever really needed in life, he taught himself.

"Here's something else y'all can try," says Baxter, handing us each a soft white strip of torn bedsheet. Whoa! Is he trying to get *us* to wear blindfolds? I don't…know if…

He quickly follows up: "The blindfold will help you *feel* the hoop. When you take eyesight out of the equation, your other senses—especially your sense of touch—will perk up." It makes total sense, though I've never thought about it before...because...why *would* I? And how did *he* think of it?!

I decide right then that there is nothing imaginable that this guy could ask me to do that I'm not willing to at least *try*...I mean, he coaxed a sacred...dance out of a plastic...*tube*, for god's sake! I tie on my strip of sheet firmly and squat, feeling around on the floor for my big, fuzzy-wuzzy circle.

Behind my blindfold, the world changes right away. No longer am I within the wide vista of outwardly manifest reality, but in a radically subjective realm, aware of only—at first—the two points where the floor meets my footsoles, and the two heavy, enfurred places where my hoop rests in both my hands. I bring the inner wall of the hoop to my lower back and press in, the way Baxter showed us. I twist my upper body as far as I can to the left, drawing the hoop back with me, then throw it to the right, nice and hard, following through with my left arm. The big hoop wavers and wobbles like the deck of a ship, but I dutifully rock back and forth, feeling the soles of my feet press into the floor in constantly changing patterns, and the hoop—swinging like the surface of the sea—stays up.

Five minutes ago, I could not hula-hoop; now I am hooping with a blindfold on. The mass of the hoop—muted by the velvety fabric—presses into me from all directions, yet self-locates around this band of sensation that spans my waist, evening itself out through the centripetal force that radiates into my core. The hoop's motion creates in me a physical center—a disambiguated column, which is the conceptual-yet-real axis of its rotation. This center is not materially real—simply being one of the inevitable aspects of the motion of a perfectly round object—but I certainly perceive it. I *feel* it.

"Okay, everybody—let's get our blindfolds on, and get inside our hoops..." Baxter's voice resonates across the room. "Spread yourselves out—Ann, Kimo, y'all can stay where you are. Let's fill up all the space..." He sounds so reassuring and dadlike. "Now, remember, I won't be blindfolded, so I'll be running interference, making sure no one bumps into each other..." Gentle laughs rumble up over the spare electronic music

35

coming through the speakers. "So don't worry about collisions. I got you." His voice is not only Southern, but *sweet*—like one note gently pressed from a piano.

I am alone in the dark with Baxter's voice. It is the best place I have visited in a long, long time. Moment by moment, my feet gain certainty on the smooth, solid floor, and the hoop goes around more steadily. *Whoop whoop whoop whoop*...I feel the rhythm establishing itself, marking time in the simplest way. The more I feel it, the more I can do it. It seems miraculous that my body can figure out so much in such a short span of time. It just gets easier and easier, with every revolution the hoop makes.

"Bring your mind to the point of contact," Baxter says over the droning track, "the place where the hoop is touching your body." Instantly, I become aware of the single, ovoid spot on the inside wall of my hoop, pressing into my torso as it revolves around me. It tugs against me, pulling me with it in a kind of spiraling wake. "This point," says Baxter, "is the place where the hoop communicates with you. The hoop talks to you through the point of contact. Whenever you feel yourself start to lose the hoop," —which is, quite honestly, starting to happen to me right now— "bring your mind back to the point of contact." I promptly return my attention back to the little oval pressing into me. As I do this, my body, syncing up with my mind's focus, shimmies just enough to reinitiate the hoop's rhythm—just enough to bump it back to a slightly quicker speed, and keep the hoop from sinking down with the force of gravity. Behind my blindfold, I grin; I have executed my first "save."

"Remember, the point of contact is always a place you can return to," Baxter intones. "It is always there. You can always connect to it, no matter what you are doing with the hoop." I let my mind again gently touch the point, this spot of moving mass, this place I can always return to.

"Now," Baxter continues, "just keep on moving with your hoops, feeling the point, and for the next few minutes I'm gonna tell y'all...a story." *Of course he's a storyteller*, I swoon, silently. *Of course he is!* "Now, I wanna be clear, here—this is a story I made up!" A few chuckles flutter up over the music. "When I was first hooping, in my blindfold, by myself in my backyard, I would start to...imagine things. I would be dancing in my hoop, and these...visions...would come to me, of these amazing hoopers, these superhero, larger-than-life figures. They seemed to me to be the original tribe, the people who might have been the first hoopers." *A myth of origin!* I exult to myself. *He's going to tell us a myth of origin!* If my crush could get any more intense right now, I cannot imagine how. It doesn't seem possible.

"And these hoopers, in this vision I saw, they were...they were *women.* This original tribe of hoopers was made up entirely of women. Strong, powerful, magical, holy women. And they practiced dancing with the hoop...as a form of meditation." I feel tears sting the backs of my eyes. *A tribe, made up entirely of women.* "And these women—they danced with the hoop in order to stay connected to that eternal rhythm, the pulse that beats behind all things. Through their dance they maintained...relationship...to this divine inner rhythm. Through their practice with the hoop, they found balance, between the inner and outer worlds." Utterly unaccountably, I think: *I am one of those women.*

"These women danced for their community, they danced to tell stories, they danced to keep that divine rhythm alive on earth. They served as healers, and...arbiters of truth. And they lived together as family. I call them the Maidan." He pronounces it 'my-*DAN.*' "And the Maidan...they lived in a time when...when women and girls were really not...*valued,* equally. This was a time when, in some families, if a baby was born and it turned out not to be a son, but a daughter—the family might, they might take that little baby...and abandon her, leave her out somewhere, to die." The room suddenly seems very quiet; only the dim drone of the background track, and the after-echo of Baxter's voice.

"And the Maidan, they could understand the language of the birds; they had learned how to communicate with them, through gesture. And so, when one of these baby girls was abandoned somewhere, the birds would fly to the Maidan, and tell them, and guide them back to her. And they would bring the baby home, and raise her...as one of their own. And so the Maidan order...was a sisterhood." *All the baby girls, who were abandoned, and left to die.* Hot tears push against the cotton weave of my blindfold, but I am NOT going to start blubbering in the middle of Baxter talking. Across the room, I hear one loud, wet sniff. I'm not alone.

"So tonight," Baxter goes on, "Tonight we are going to practice the dance of Two Birds. This was how the Maidan learned to speak with the birds. The Maidan would *trace* their flight—they would watch birds in the sky and, with their hands, follow their flight. So…behind your blindfold, in your mind's eye…I want you to picture two birds, flying."

I feel my hoop lightly push-pulling me in space as I focus on the vision of two birds swooping through the air. "And as you see these birds," Baxter says, "as you see their flight across the sky, try lifting your hands, and following them." *Metaphor!* I shout to myself, my crush on Baxter eclipsing all crushes that have ever existed in the history of time. *A man who speaks metaphor!!!* I lift up my hands and move them lightly through space. I feel the air molecules hitting my palms, arms, fingers—swirling across my skin like water. The curlicues of moving air seem to suggest movements to my hands. Cautiously, I let my hands follow the filigree of new sensations, the images of two birds dancing before me.

"Take up space!" Baxter shouts from across the room. "Expand, reach, grow, *fly!*" Another song comes over the speakers, a song with a slow beat and a beautiful female voice. For once, I don't have a plan. I'm just here, in space, moving my body with the rhythm of my big mother-hoop. My hands glide easily through the newly tactile air, sweeping and diving amidst the swirling nanoparticles. The voice and the rhythm and the birds move me, they move through me, curving my arms and hands into unexpected shapes.

"Let yourself *feel!*" calls Baxter. "Let yourself *feel* what is happening! Feel your hoop, your hands, the air moving across your body! Let it *lift* you!" My body continues to pump the hoop—*whoosh whoosh whoosh*—while my hands rise into the air without effort, as though of their own volition, spiraling through the infinite currents of air surrounding my moving body. The voice over the speakers sings:

You can fly fly fly fly—
You can live or you can die…

"*Feel* the point of contact, *feel* the space around you, *feel* your birds flying!" Baxter's voice vibrates with joy. My heart, my entire body springs open, alive to every ripple of air hitting my body, to every wave of harmonic vibration touching my eardrums, to every echo of rhythm resounding through the floor beneath my feet. My hands swing, curve, dive freely through a limitless sky.

"There is no ceiling!" Baxter cries. "No limits…no boundaries…only sky!" he shouts to us. "*No* ceiling! *No* boundaries! *Only sky…*"

I haven't once thought about my ex, or the pain, or cigarettes, or the inevitability of beer. Instead, I feel my body unfurl into the rippling air—my feet rooted to the floor, holding me down, while my hands and arms reach ever higher, exploring the entirely new space around me. Bright sensations shiver over my skin—as my body moves, the air moves against me like wind, lifting me up, up and out. *I'm dancing,* I think to myself. I'm dancing with a single shape—the circle—and an image: two soaring birds. And suddenly I understand an altogether new truth: *Metaphor can be danced, too.* As my feet rock and my core sways and my hands sail, utterly free. My blindfold is wet through and my lips tremble now and I don't even care because *metaphor can be danced, too.* This random-ass hot guy had, by some miracle, managed to understand that. There was a sacred dance inside a hula-hoop, and Baxter knew it, somehow. He had figured it out. And then he tossed that unmistakably life-preserving shape towards me, in total darkness, and told me a story, and gave me a metaphor. And now I, too, am flying.

VIII.

Feeling

"Let's not forget that the little emotions are the great captains of our lives and we obey them without realizing it."

— Vincent van Gogh

Do you know how to feel?

This is a technical question.

* * *

The first time I spun the hoop around my body was also the first time I caught an inkling that *feeling* could be an experience distinct from *thought*—that these phenomena are not, in fact, one in the same thing... not one single relentless self-contained, self-referential mashup of raw sensation and the overpowering, compulsively verbalized desire to *understand*. At some point very early in life—as I was carefully constructing a calm, reasonable persona to serve as the unmistakable foil to my brother's barely-regulated wildness—I had decided, without consciously intending to, that the cause of every emotion must be, above all, instantly ascertained and internally explained…this was the surest path to liberation from the terrible sway that emotions held over one's being. Any emotion that shocked or overwhelmed me with its unfamiliarity or intensity must be—above all—*understood,* which is to say *internally transmuted into words*, as swiftly as possible. That was my unstated but very closely held philosophy, from which I did not ever stray, although I did not even comprehend that it existed.

* * *

Scholars who study emotion are still far from agreeing about what it actually *is.* It is widely concurred that emotion is "complex" and that it consists of several components: mental, physiological, behavioral, et al. But in every example of emotion, there appears one irreducible feature: *subjectivity.* Someone must be *feeling* emotion in order for it to occur. Emotion must happen *to* someone, or *within* someone: "someone" being a living, perceiving, embodied human person.

However, the subjective experience of emotion does not seem to enjoy any kind of status in our culture. Being "in your feelings"—a comment that appears with startling frequency on Twitter—is understood not as a compassionate acknowledgment of this peculiar burden of the human condition, but as a blunt and shaming insult. Whenever anyone displays a strong emotion in public, you can count on a quick interventional appeal to "calm down."

I was brought up in a well-to-do Southern WASPy culture that prized self-control and the suppression and containment of emotion. While my parents had evolved a huge distance from their own Victorian "children-are-seen-and-not-heard" parents, I still received the message that emotion was something that adults and good children were able to *control*—and that it was crucially important to learn how to do so.

However, when we suppress and deny our emotions—when we refuse to feel—we limit our capacity to know ourselves. If we do not know what we feel, we cannot understand what we want, why we do what we do, or who—in fact—we are.

IX.

June, 1975

"Don't you smile."

It is my grandmother's voice—our favorite grandparent, provider of unlimited Coca-Cola and ice cream. We visit our dad's parents every summer for a week, running through their tiny bungalow at top speed until our grandfather—whom we call "Guy"—yells at us from his recliner to cut it out. Guy is crabby and intimidating, but Grandmama is intensely beloved by every grandchild.

We like to play the game where we sit across from her, maintaining steady eye contact, and try with all our might not to laugh, or smile. "*Dohhhn...cheeew...smmaaal,*" she says in a low voice, her face immobile. Grandmama absolutely never cracks. We smirk, quiver, fidget, and finally explode with laughter while her face remains absolutely still. "Do it again!" we shout, euphoric. She will play it with us as long as we want.

Guy will sometimes let us sit on his lap and play one of the scary games, where we trace the outline of his lips with one finger while he makes a deep growling sound way down in his throat. "Rrrrrrrrrrrrr-rrrrrrrrrr," he growls. "Rrrrrrrrrrrrrrrrrrrrrrrrrrrrrrrrrrrrrrrrrrrrrrrrrrrrrrrrrrrr-rrOOOOOOOAAAAWWW!" Suddenly his creepy pink dentures leap halfway out of his mouth with a loud roar. We scream and shudder in anguished delight. *"Do it again! Do it again!"*

Sometimes, when the house is full of cousins and we are all running and trying to bang on the piano right behind him, Guy will announce, "Arright now, it's time to play Guy's *favorite game*." We jump with glee and scream: "CHILDREN HUSH!!! Y'ALL LET'S PLAY CHILDREN HUSH!!!" It's a game Guy made up just for us. We race back to his bedroom all the way at the back of the house—we only play Children Hush on Guy's tall and uncomfortable bed, where we are never otherwise allowed. We all arrange ourselves on top of the bedspread so that everybody can fit, and then lie absolutely still and quiet for as long as we can possibly stand it. The adults remain in the front room, talking and laughing and drinking soft drinks, while we shush one another urgently. "Stop it, y'all! Be *quiet!* We're playing *Children Hush!*"

* * *

May, 1977

I am standing in the front hall, crying hysterically. I am seven years old. My Shetland Sheepdog, Honey, is lying in the street in front of our house. She has just been hit by a car and killed. My mother will not let me go outside to see her.

My other grandmother, my mother's mother, is visiting from South Carolina. She is not effusive and affectionate like my other Grandmama, though she clearly loves us. She never wears dresses or lipstick and lives alone in a spare ranch house where she has few visitors. When we come visit, she will allow us each night after dinner one bowl of ice milk (she doesn't buy ice cream) and two cookies. Our dad's mom will let us eat the entire half gallon container of ice cream, if we want. With this grandmother, we play Go Fish, Crazy 8s, and double solitaire, facing each other for hours across the olive green card table. After our allotted daily hour of TV (our dad's mom will let us stay up and watch Johnny Carson if we want), we might read from her complete Time/Life science library. She loves nature and is often out in the yard gardening, or raking leaves. If we are there, we have to help her.

I run up to my room to cry on my bed. Grandmama knocks on the door and comes in. She has never come into my room to visit me before. She comes over and sits on the edge of my bed. "Now, you need to stop crying, Annie," she says kindly and firmly. "You're a big girl, now." I can't even respond to her. I'm hyperventilating into my pillow. *Honey...*

"You're too big to cry," she continues, matter-of-factly. "You know, I had dogs, too, when I was a little girl." I keep wailing; I can't understand why she is trying to talk to me right now. "I had a little dog with brown and white spots. He was tiiiiny and he had a little stump tail. And he would wait for me, every day, at the back door, and his little stump tail would go *bopbopbop* against the porch." I am so shocked that she is telling me something about herself, about her life as a little girl, that I forget I'm crying.

"What was h-h-his name?" I ask, my breath still heaving.

"We called him Spodeeboats!" she says, clapping her hands together. This is such a funny name that I giggle a little, in spite of myself.

"Who were your other dogs?" I ask, thinking I will find out a lot about her life as a girl. She regales me for an hour with story after story of all her childhood dogs, until my tears have dried up and disappeared, and Honey's body has been picked up from the street outside, and the sun has started to sink low in the sky.

Before dark I go outside to join in a game of badminton with a few other neighborhood kids. As I set up a serve, my neighbor Danny says, "Hey, are you okay? I heard Honey got hit today." I feel a wrongness deep inside me, as though something utterly unallowable has been said. I can remember the terrible feelings of earlier in the day, but they seem to have been folded and tucked away somewhere I can't reach. "Yeah..." I say, looking away from him and thwacking the birdie into the air. I wish Danny hadn't asked me about it. I wish he hadn't mentioned Honey at all.

* * *

July, 1977

I have just come home from my first trip in a plane. I flew down to Tupelo, Mississippi, all by myself, to visit my cousins for two weeks. When Mom picks me up at the airport in her yellow car, she is alone. "Where's Daddy?" I ask, after hugging her tightly. Both my parents had come to the airport to drop me off when I got on the plane. "You'll see him a little later," Mom responds.

As we ride down the highway, Mom glances in the rearview mirror at me, belted into my seat in the back. She is wearing a bright green dress with tiny white polka-dots on it. She isn't talking very much. "Where's *Daddy*?" I ask again. "Why didn't he come with you?"

"Well," Mom says slowly, looking at me again in the rearview, "Annie, honey—Daddy and I, have decided—that we don't want to live together anymore." The last part slips quickly out of her mouth, her voice shivering as it races to finish the sentence. What she is saying can't be true. We can't not all live together! Where's my Daddy??!

"Where...where is he?"

"Well, Daddy—has an apartment, now, and you"— Mom is holding back her tears, watching the road, checking in the mirror to catch my eyes— "you and Greg will go there and spend nights with him, there."

"He didn't leave us!" I yell at the back of my mother's head. *"No he didn't!"* Huge hot tears burst from my eyes as I begin howling at the top of my voice.

"Honey, I know it's hard...to understand, *right now*, but you and Greg will—"

"He wouldn't leave us!!! He wouldn't!!!!! HE WOULDN'T!!!" I scream at my mother. My father would never leave me. He would never leave my brother.

"Honey..." Mom tries to tell me that I will see Daddy all the time, I will have another home to go to, we will have more time together.

"NO!!!! NO!!!! NO!!!!!!!" I scream with all my might. I refuse to believe that he has left us. He would just not ever do that. He *wouldn't*.

When we pull into the driveway I do not wait for my mother. I unbuckle my seat belt and bolt out of the car, through the front door, up the stairs, into my parents' bedroom, and over to my father's large armoire. I tear open the double doors. And high above me, where I can't reach, are all his empty wooden coathangers, dangling like bones. All his suits are gone, all his shirts and sweaters. *He wouldn't leave us. He would never leave us.*

I run screaming and sobbing into my bedroom and throw myself face-down on my bed. "*NO!!!!!!!!*" I scream again and again. "*NO!!!! DADDY!!!!!*" Mom comes in, sits on my bed, and tries to talk to me. She tries to tell me how much Daddy loves me, how it isn't my fault, how we will be able to see him even more than we do now. I just scream and cry, banging my face into my pillow. "**NO NO NO!!!!!!!!**" He hasn't left us...he *wouldn't.*

I cry and cry. My breathing is all jerky. Mom keeps trying to talk to me, to tell me it's going to be okay. I can't hear her over my wailing. **DADDY!!!!!!** She walks out of the room, but comes right back in a minute later.

"Annie, look—" she says. Against my will I peek up from my pillow. She is holding up a piece of yellow flowered fabric I have admired from her sewing area. "I'll make you a dress out of this; it will be so pretty!" I love that fabric—with tiny blue and orange and green buds all over it in a wiggly pattern. "I'll make it into a sundress for you," she says, "with a little kerchief to match!" I'm looking at the yellow fabric, bunched in her hands. I imagine a long dress, down to my ankles, like a grown-up's. My jerking breath starts to slow down. "Can it be"—(hiccup)—"a long dress?"

Mom smiles at me. She is proud of me for being able to calm down. "Of course, honey!" she says brightly. "We'll make it long, like a big-girl dress."

I breathe heavily but evenly. "A big-girl dress," I repeat.

"You'll look so pretty," she says, smoothing back my hair.

* * *

August, 1988

It is early morning. My brother drove in from college late last night. He and my mother and I are at the hospital, along with Mary Jean, my father's girl-friend of the last year and a half. We are all crammed into my father's small private room. In a few minutes, they will come and get him for the biopsy.

My brother and I stand on either side of my father's narrow hospital bed, holding his hands and looking awkwardly down at him, suddenly small beneath us. Greg chats with him gamely. I barely speak; I can't think what to say. Mom and Mary Jean, meeting for the first time, exchange pleasantries with the bulletproof tact learned from Southern mothers. My father, always the sustainer of conversation, is unusually quiet—he sits upright in the bed, looking confusingly like a small boy staying home sick from school. He responds to my brother but doesn't initiate any of his own questions or comments; I don't think of the fact that he has probably already been partially sedated for surgery. Mary Jean, a sharp-minded and amiable quiltmaker from the mountains, jumps in to share some of the details of the biopsy plan: it will take a few hours; we will all wait here to hear from the doctors after they complete the procedure.

Though my brother goes to college only 90 minutes away, we seldom see him back here at home. He has a full schedule of classes and fronts a band which plays nearly every weekend. Greg sings, plays guitar, and writes the songs. We have grown up singing with our dad, who plays guitar and a little bit of banjo. While Daddy is only a passable guitarist, his tenor singing voice is sweet and clear. He is a huge fan of the "cosmic cowboy" style out of Austin, and owns the entire vinyl catalogs of his heroes, Jimmy Buffett and Jerry Jeff Walker. Greg has, predictably, moved in a different direction, playing Smiths-infused rock & roll to college audiences. But despite these aesthetic distinctions, my brother is still living my father's closely held dream of being a traveling musician. I stand poised to live out another, more conventional dream: ascending into the highest echelons of academia.

A team of orderlies sweeps in to transfer my father to a trolley. There is a sudden confusion. Mom leaves the room to give them space. My brother and I stand back, watching them move my father—as if he is unable to stand and walk—from the bed onto the rolling stretcher. When he's secured, they back out, wheeling him behind so he faces us. Mary Jean waits out in the hallway to accompany him to the OR. Just before they whisk him out of sight, he raises one hand in a faint wave.

The sun has not yet risen—the sky outside is still dark. My brother sits down at the foot of the hospital bed, his head still peering out the open doorway from which our father has just vanished. I stand in the corner, frozen. I do not understand what to think or say or feel. I'm looking at my brother, at the back of his head. I see that his back is shaking. He swivels around to look at me, and I see the tears shining on his face.

"All while I was talking to him I was just…fighting back crying—" he chokes, shaking his head rapidly as if to clear it.

I just stand there, in the corner of the room, staring at him witlessly. Inside, I am an unreachable blankness. I do not comprehend, I do not cry, I just stand silently. This isn't happening. He continues to weep, bending his head into his hand. I don't know what to do. Mom hasn't come back yet—she probably went down the hall to the bathroom. I have to say something to him—I have to do something. The room is clogged with the sound of his sniffles and sighs and my stone silence. I have never comforted him before—I have never had to. I have to go up to him. I have to do something. I have to.

In a trance of emptiness, I walk slowly up to my brother and place my hands on his silky blond hair. I let my hands slip across his head, petting him like a cat. I don't know what else to do. He turns and grabs me around the waist in a powerful hug. I stand motionless, without expression, my hands resting on my brother's skull as he sobs and sobs into my side. I can't feel anything. And because I feel nothing, I know: there is definitely something wrong with me.

* * *

Hours later, a doctor appears in the doorframe, summoning the four of us out into the hallway and into an adjacent conference room. A long table almost entirely fills the room, which is jammed full of stacks of extra chairs, boxes of papers, and stray hospital machinery. There is a long blackboard along one wall. We squeeze into the four available chairs. I am at the end, next to Mary Jean. Doctors line the opposite side of the table, the blackboard behind them sharpening the white of their immaculate coats. The one doctor we know, a friend of my father's, stands next to the blackboard, holding a piece of chalk. He has big Buddy Holly glasses and a large bald patch. I remember his name from the church membership directory: Dr. McEllvoy.

He begins to speak, glancing over his shoulder as he simultaneously starts drawing on the blackboard a crude rendering of my father's head. *Malignancy tumor glioblastoma anaplastic ganglia advanced inoperable.* In the middle of my father's chalked skull, he draws a hulking, amoebic shape. We sit for seconds in a vacuous silence. My brother's voice is the first sound:

"How long does he have?"

Dr. McEllvoy looks at us for a moment without saying anything. He swings back to the marked-up blackboard. "On the outside," he says, raising one hand in a bizarre half-wave, "two years. In the worst case"—he forces himself to turn around and look at us—"three to six months."

"Three to six *months*?" my brother echoes, his voice shrinking. His face crumples as he and Mom throw their arms around each other, their sobs shattering the air in the silent room. Mary Jean and I turn to each other and hug quickly. We tear up lightly but do not break down or sob. I cannot feel that this is happening. It is happening too fast.

We walk across the hall to my father's room. He lies flat and still in the hospital bed. They have shaved back part of his hair for the biopsy, just above his forehead, so his hairline looks suddenly and weirdly receded. My brother rushes over to him, bending to embrace him as his tears fall on our father's chest. "You're the…best…daddy…anyone ever…had," he howls, gasping between the words. My father cries very softly and pats him on the back, saying, "I love you, buddy." But his voice is strikingly hoarse and doesn't sound like him.

My brother moves to the side and I bend to hug my father, cool tears seeping from my eyes. My mind is a white emptiness. I don't know what to say to him. What can I say?! "You're the best…Pop…" I sputter, instantly horrified that I cannot think of anything else to say and am just parroting my brother. Everyone must be able to see that I do not love him—everyone must be able to tell. I'm so sickened by myself but there isn't anywhere to go or anything to do because I must hug my father right now and tell him I love him. "I love you," I say, praying he won't notice how abnormal I am, how cold, perverse, inhuman. And in his new, strange, hoarse voice, he—of course—says it back to me.

X.

Second Current

Return is the movement of the Tao.
Yielding is the way of the Tao.

— Lao Tzu

Every hooper has what might be called their "favorite" direction—one way of hooping that is distinctly easier than its opposite. For most hoopers, this is to the *left* (shout out to all my righty hoopers! We are few but we exist!!). Most of us, when we are hooping on the core (i.e., when the hoop is horizontally rotating around the waist, shoulders, or legs) feel distinctly more comfortable when the hoop is going in our *favorite*, i.e., easier, direction. With Baxter, in his poetic hoop lexicon, we called this our *First Current*.

We all also have what we might call our "second-favorite direction"—i.e., the opposite of our favorite direction. Baxter called this our

Second Current, and established a guideline: whenever we dropped the hoop, we must begin again by spinning it in the opposite direction. In this way, we ensured that we would get at least somewhat equal time practicing in that awkward, frustrating, weird-feeling, less-comfortable direction. We all, of course, hated it at first...and—over time—we all grew to understand what an invaluable gift this teaching was.

Learning to hula-hoop taught me that I could do things I thought I could not do. Hooping in my Second Current taught me that I could not only do things I thought to be impossible—I could also get better at things that felt irredeemably awkward and "wrong." With Baxter, we practiced every technique in both currents, with both hands—never limiting ourselves to just our "good side." Hooping in Second Current from the very beginning meant that, as my hooping journey went on, I was never consigned to a predetermined path—I could always pivot in either direction, flip to my opposite current, use my non-dominant hand. This new world of dance was equally open to me in every conceivable direction. Eventually, I made these transitions without thinking.

If you are just starting to hoop (which—I admit—I hope you are), understand that any awkwardness you are willing to face now will return to you in grace later on in your journey. Every time you are willing to pick up your hoop from the floor and spin it in the opposite, less-comfortable, less-fun-feeling direction, know that you are embracing your Shadow. And you are dancing with it. And the more you dance with this Shadow, the more you allow its energy to permeate your body, the more grace you will feel as the two of you melt together into one dancer, one dance.

XI.

September, 2006

It has been just over a year since I took my first hoop class with Baxter. Although I was ready to spend the rest of my life with him that night after my first hoop class—it didn't quite work out that way. Because he (of course) already had a girlfriend.

She was an "aspiring journalist" who crept around filming our hoop class one night a few weeks later, trying strenuously to stay out of view like some kind of anthropologist. I didn't realize what the deal was until nearly the end of class, when Baxter placed a hand on her back and left it there. The force of my shock and shame rendered me unable to return to the class. It was too much, with the ongoing solicited-rejection-fest I continued to engage in with my ex. Luckily, I had bought the leopard-print hoop that first night and kept on hooping with it, every couple of weeks or so, on my back porch. So, although it can't be said that I progressed, I didn't forget absolutely everything Baxter had taught me.

Then, a few weeks ago, he sent me a friend request on MySpace, which I instantly accepted. A friendly message followed, then another, then another ("He's certainly being nice," I thought), until suddenly there was a fourth, slightly longer message from him saying, "Hey, I didn't know you were seeing Dave...he's a great guy, congratulations." Dave was my ex-boyfriend—the heartless dumper—but Dave was *also* the name of his good friend with whom I'd been hooking up randomly in a half-hearted effort to get over the other Dave. So, when I got this message, I had no idea which Dave he was talking about.

"Hi! Thanks for writing! I'm actually NOT dating Dave and I would like to hang out with -you- if you're available," is how my fourth Myspace reply began. About fifteen minutes after I sent this reply, I started to panic that he wouldn't receive it before he forgot about me entirely and got focused on someone else (this was before we had the internet on our cell phones). So I called the bar where he worked. He wasn't there, but his co-worker—who knew me—gave me his cell number. I called him right away, repeating my nakedly obvious message almost verbatim. We drunkenly hooked up that night and just kept on hanging throughout the summer. I quickly forgot all about my ex. Baxter is my boyfriend now.

Kimo has also kept up with hooping, and over the last couple of months the three of us have been meeting most afternoons over at Baxter's place to practice. He has a large backyard with space for us all to have our own hoop "patch." There are now three large brown circles in the deep green grass where we have worn it away with our dancing.

We come here to hoop almost every afternoon. Baxter hauls out the waist-high 70s speakers, trailing their coppery cables, and sets them up by the back door. We duck into the living room to toke from a large glass bong before beginning our movement. I've barely ever smoked weed before; many years ago, when I was living in India, I smoked regularly (tobacco, ganja, beedees) with my Bengali boyfriend and his group of friends. Though it was an overwhelmingly positive experience, sitting around their house listening to tapes of Bob Marley and Toots & the Maytalls and laughing to the point of tears, I didn't continue toking when I came back stateside. This was the mid-90s, and my college town was all about grunge rock, Marlboro reds, and PBR. I can count on one hand the times I have gotten stoned between then and now.

But the plant has proved a miraculous companion to dancing in the sun for hours these summer afternoons. I feel the movement of my body anew—I can find spaces around me I've never felt before, I can move my body in ways I have never been able to. I feel as if I live in a whole new body: a dancing body. A body that can move at once with both greater precision and greater freedom. A body that senses itself in space, a body that moves through space with grace and ease (as well as—let's face it—agonizing awkwardness).

After we've hooped for a couple of hours, we will often sit and talk... sometimes for another couple of hours. Baxter has fit right into Kimo's and my omnitopical dynamic. We start off talking about what new moves we learned or perfected that day, and end up on the Upanishads, or Ted Kennedy, or "Ways of Seeing." We have just finished our day's hoop practice, and are sitting on Baxter's back stoop. Baxter and I are each having a can of Miller Lite. Kimo doesn't drink, but is smoking one of the American Spirits he likes to ironically enjoy. Over the last couple of months, my drinking and tobacco use have declined precipitously.

"How was y'all's hoop?" asks Baxter, always eager to hear our reports of struggle and success.

"Pretty great, man!" Kimo says, jouncing up and down on his feet in excitement. Hooping always gets him super-pumped. "I got that...Sky Angle. I got it down good this time." He means hooping facing the sky, with the hoop at a steep angle.

"I saw you working on that!" Baxter grins hugely. "You are *kil-ling* that shit, man. For real."

"Ya think so?" Kimo's large brown eyes pop open with sincere surprise. Despite his rock-solid self-assurance in most situations, he is a humble hooper—learning slowly and painstakingly, working on the simplest techniques for hours, facing away from us much of the time.

"Hell yes," Bax rejoins. "You're all the way out of the Belief phase. Now it'll be a steady build into Strength." In Baxter's hoop classes, he has a concept he calls Belief-Strength-Grace. It's a theory about how we master hoop moves. First, he says, we see someone pull off a move—so we know it can be done, we know that it is possible: that's Belief. The first time we nail that move ourselves—the first time we complete it, no matter how awkwardly—we have entered the Strength phase. This is where we can drill the move over and over again so that we can execute it reliably. And the first time we execute the move without thinking—the first time the motion rolls from our body with the effortless action the Taoists call *wu wei*—we have entered Grace.

"You looked awesome, K," I aver. "Smooth, fluid, and a nice even angle. No blooping over to one side."

"You're finding your *feet,* man," says Bax. In class he is always exhorting us to feel our feet, to learn how our feet affect the hoop's rhythm. One of his favorite class mantras is: *The whole body hoops.*

"It's the ground," Kimo replies. "The dirt. I feel different hooping on the earth. I like it better than that fake wood floor in the studio." Kimo doesn't come to class every week like I do. He prefers to navigate his own hoop journey. He'll listen to Baxter the first time he describes a move or trick, but from then on, he'll be trying it his own way.

"It does feel different out here," I muse, looking out over the yard of dark green grass and its tin shed, scraggly wire fence, and three wide circles of packed dirt.

"Yes it does," echoes Bax, taking a swallow of Miller Lite.

"I was even doing it in Second Current," Kimo elaborates, the corner of his mouth curling up into a proud but unwilled smile, his brilliance and authority in most arenas of life having made him self-conscious of boasting.

"Ah *yeah,* bro!" Baxter is tickled.

"I never was able to do the Sky Angle to the right," Kimo says. He is, like most, a lefty hooper. "Ya know, I really like that Second Current as a concept," he continues, Canadianly rounding and stretching the first syllable of the last word: **cohhn**-*cept.* Bax and I often tease him about his Canadian pronunciations. "It gives you…the opportunity to find beginner's mind, again and again."

"Exactly!" I affirm. "It's like a slate-clearing. It feels so impossible, but then you start to find all this extra space."

"Second Current takes you into the places you don't want to go," observes Bax.

"Like Jung's Shadow," I say.

"Totally!" Kimo's face lights up. His affect tends to oscillate between Know-It-All Professor and Excited Five-Year-Old. Much like—

perhaps—my own. "The Shadow recognizes that *all* parts make up the whole…not just the visible, or the preferable."

"Or the easy," Baxter cracks, making us chuckle for a second.

Kimo mulls on, crushing his spent cig in the dirt: "It's a lot like the Four Directions." He means the circular Lakota symbol that accounts for all creation. "The image allows us to understand the wholeness of what we see, while recognizing that—as we look in one direction—we can't see any of the others. But they all still exist. And they complete, and…*balance*, one another." He jumps up and pulls another cigarette out of the pack, ripping off the filter and paper until there is just a little pile of tobacco in his palm. "We have the East," he says, walking toward the sagging fence, "which is where the light comes--" and here he bends down, setting a little mound of tobacco on the ground and lighting it. He waits a moment as the smoke rises, then walks farther away, toward the line of cinderblocks that divide this property from the neighbor's. "And the South," he says, bending and lighting another tobacco pile, "where we get warmth, and growth." We watch the gray ribbon of smoke curl up around him. "The West!" he smiles, walking toward my patch, which abuts the gravel side street. "From here we get darkness, wetness, the underground, the Shadow." I smell the burning tobacco through the warm late-summer air. And he walks back toward the stoop, making one last small pile in front of us with the rest of the dried tobacco. "And the North," he continues, "where we come to know cold, and absence, and emptiness."

As Kimo bends down again to light the little pile of tobacco, I see a strip of the bald spot on the back of his head, usually covered by the way he gathers his long hair into a ponytail. Though Kimo is in his early 40s, this isn't a regular middle-aged-guy bald patch. It's a perfectly square section of hairless skin where he received targeted radiation when he was diagnosed at age 29 with the slowest-growing type of brain tumor, *oligodendroglioma*. He has been living with this brain cancer for the last 13 years.

The typical life expectancy of a person with oligodendroglioma is 10 to 12 years. Kimo has already had his skull cut open twice. The last time was just over a year ago. His ex-girlfriend flew in from California to help him through the surgery. Within a few weeks, he was back on his feet, working, teaching, making art, hooping. "Recently underwent brain surgery for cancer" would be among the last things anyone would ever guess about him.

Kimo stands and steps back, observing the strands of smoke as they unfurl from the tiny haystack of tobacco. Baxter and I sit, watching with him. We have been talking a lot lately about ritual, how absent it is from our contemporary lives. "Why don't we have a fire tonight, y'all?" Baxter proposes. We've been talking about having a fire for weeks, but even the evenings have been hot. Today feels a little bit cooler.

"Yeah, let's do that!" Kimo agrees. "Tonight will be perfect."

"YESSSS," I whoop, high-fiving them both in turn. Tonight will be perfect.

* * *

We reunite a few hours later, after the long and late sunset. It has gotten perceptibly cooler; I wear jeans and a second layer, Bax and Kimo wear hoodies. It's dark in the backyard. We don't speak much as we transfer the firewood from my trunk out to the stone circle Baxter has assembled. The big speakers drone some chill electronica—for me, an entirely new form of music. We pile the wood and kindling next to the stones, and I grab the paper bag full of old newspapers from my backseat. Baxter and I crouch next to the circle, twisting pieces of newspaper into fluffy rolls which we poke into the pyramid of wood Kimo is building. After a while, we are ready to light.

Kimo flicks his lighter around the base of the pyramid, and the paper twists catch fire, flickering through the airy cage of wood. In two or three minutes, the whole pile is aflame.

We sit in folding chairs, watching the fire. Baxter pulls out a glass pipe, packs it, and takes a puff. We pass it among us, listening to the pop and crackle of the new flames. The night sky is a beautiful, deep blue, flecked with tiny bright stars.

After a time, Baxter stands and picks up his black hoop from the grass. He's still gazing at the fire, but he now has the hoop in his hands, and is moving with it. The light from the fire bounces off him, showing his arms move the hoop at lightning speed. I can't even tell what he is doing with the hoop—my skills haven't caught up to off-body hooping yet. I can only rotate my huge, massy hoop around my core—it's too big to hold in my hands.

In Baxter's arms, the black hoop moves with a quick liquidity, like a snake. It actually looks like he is wrestling with a live black snake right now. The hoop twists and roils between his arms, around his body, up in the air, behind him, and back again. I'm riveted—I can't stop watching the poetry of his movement. HOW did he figure out how to do all these things with the hoop??!!? I just can't fathom…he seems to me a magical entity, an enchanted being. His arms thread through the hoop, and out again, and then he stands the hoop upright, balancing it on the back of one hand…

I take a moment to make sure my mouth isn't hanging open. It's… just so…*amazing*…that he can do all this with a hoop. I mean…*how????* He is just…*guiding* the hoop; it moves almost of its own accord…he has brought it to life, he has made the hoop into a living being.

Amidst all this inner fanfare, a rogue thought creeps: *Why is he even WITH me?* Baxter is (I've checked on the new video sharing site, You-Tube) THE MOST jaw-dropping male hooper in existence today. Nobody even compares. I'm just a crappy beginner, stiff and ungainly…I can't do *any* off-body yet, and it will be years before I can manage leg hooping. Why in the *hell* would he be wasting his time with *me*? I can barely even shoulder hoop!

I notice that these insecure thoughts have begun to balloon within me, taking up more and more space. I know I'm not as good a hooper as Bax—how could I be?!? I only just started! And yet, the revelation of my inadequacy comes on like a tsunami—before I'm fully aware that the wave has begun, I am drowning. *You'll never be as good as he is,* some voice whispers evilly. *Never…you'll never be…you'll never be.* I've never imagined that I could be as good as Bax, but somehow this thoughtfeeling pierces me like a blade. *What's the point of hooping?* says the voice with malevolence. *You'll never be shit.* But I love hooping! I don't want to stop! I want to be with Baxter! *You can never be that good,* the voice cackles. *You'll just be a fucking embarrassment to him.*

I begin to realize that this flurry of self-doubt is threatening to derail our beautiful evening. I can't give in to this sinking anxiety—I have to figure out how to change course. And my eye falls on my own leopard-print hoop, lying in the grass next to me. *Of course,* I exult inwardly. *I'll just HOOP!* The act of hooping never fails to bring about the purest elation. All I need to do is start! I stand, grab the hoop off the ground, and set it into motion around my waist. Now all I have to do is hoop, and wait to be covered by the blanket of euphoria that attends every single hoop session.

Except, this does not happen. I am not blanketed by euphoria. Instead, my feeling of anxious dread seems to deepen, with every single revolution the hoop makes. *Whoosh...whoosh...whoosh...*every time it goes around, the inexplicable feeling of awfulness seems to increase by an exponent of 100. *Whoosh...whoosh...whoosh...whoosh...*my insides are dropping, falling through a mysterious expanse. I feel the hoop around me, yet what it is touching does not seem to be the outermost border of my body, but rather a precipitously expanding sense of dread—a whirlpool of darkness that seems to originate not from any logical, perceptible source, but from some frighteningly unreachable place within. But, why? How? It's happening too fast for my questions, for my definitions, for my capacity to understand. I'm just being sucked headlong into this vortex of what seems, what feels, exactly like terror.

Determined not to allow this weird schwerve to negate our beautiful night, I decide that I absolutely have to—I *must*—change what I am feeling. Since every rotation of the hoop appears to be worsening this baffling slide into a sourceless dread I cannot even name, I conclude that I have to, at least, get away from Baxter and Kimo. I can't risk having my new boyfriend witness me degenerate into quivering hysteria for no reason whatsoever. I have to go inside—I have to *leave,* I have to get *away.* Abruptly I drop the hoop into the grass beneath me—*Fop!*—and, without saying a word to Baxter or Kimo, begin marching towards the back door, which shines in the night like a golden beacon. Though I want to very badly, I refuse to allow myself to run.

I yank open the rickety door, expecting the warm glow of electric light and sense of enclosure to immediately soothe the incomprehensible terror that is building inside me, second by second. Instead, as I hear the door snap shut behind me, the quaking, unplumbable, nauseous feeling spikes unbearably. *What is happening??!* My vigilance to discern what I am experiencing and place it within a coherent context suddenly flaps out somewhere far behind me, receding like a tissue in a hurricane wind. The deep well of horror that has opened to me grows larger, larger—its wide mouth hanging open in ghastly, hysterical laughter.

I break into a run, absurd rationales ticking uselessly through my head: *There's no one here...I'm alone...I don't need to run...no one's here....* But this recognition—that I am alone in the house, that no one else is here—only serves to inflame the abject terror that now possesses me entirely. I gallop through the house like a deranged madwoman, bashing into doorframes as I try, try, try to get in front of what is happening. *What is happening?* I can't make any sense, I can't comprehend it—I'm just *running,* through the *house,* like a goddamn *loon,* it's making no *sense,* I cannot *stop it. Stop it stop it stop it you must stop you must stop now* The more thoughts buzz up into my head, the more terrified I become, because nothing makes any *sense.* Though I am all too keenly aware that there is no one behind me, chasing me through the house with an upraised ax, this is precisely the feeling that engulfs my being with the blood-stopping clarity of truth.

The voice cackles in my head: *fucking nuts you aren't even sane look at you running from nothing running like a baby from nothing nothing at all*

I reach the living room at the front of the house to find that there is nowhere else to go. I can't, I can't, I can't think of opening the front door—I can't think of going out *there.* There is no negotiable space in my mind. There is only this white-out of pure terror. Of nothing. Yet, with every nanosecond that passes, it grows worse. I actually begin to run around and around the perimeter of the room, looking for some way...*out,* some way of getting away from this horrifying nothingness.

There's no way out, the voice jeers, in the fond, hopeless tone of a seasoned serial killer. *There's just no way.* I would like to cry, I would like to scream out in terror, but there is no way to make a sound. I try to open my mouth, to yell something to someone, but it just opens and closes, a cave of emptiness. I can't, I can't, I just *can't* get away from it. I can't, because it's *nothing*—nothing at all.

As I stagger ludicrously around the empty living room, a single pin-prick of understanding cuts through the consuming horror: If there is, in fact, nothing here, then all I am experiencing is the *feeling* of fear. *This is fear,* I say to myself. *This is just the feeling of fear.* And I realize that be-cause it is only a feeling, all it is asking of me is *to be felt.* So I decide—be-cause I really have no other choice that I can perceive—that I will simply *allow myself* to feel it. I will open to and surrender to this fear. I will stop trying to get away from this feeling and just *feel* it.

The instant I make this decision, the full force of Fear blasts into me with the power of a million black holes, kicking me backwards like an explosion. I fall through space; I am eradicated; I do not exist. *It is just like dying,* my mind says, from some now-faraway place, as I plunge into the emptiest oblivion. *The fear of death is death itself. The fear of death is death itself.*

Yet, a fraction of a second later, I find myself lying half-on, half-off the couch, staring up at the bare ceiling bulb as the feeling that has just annihilated me begins to drain from my body, exactly like water from a bathtub. Too stunned to move, I feel some gravitational force pull the feeling down my whole body and out through my footsoles. Within sec-onds, it has drained from me entirely.

I lie there, blinking up at the tiny sphere of light. I have, however im-probably, just triumphed over a mysterious and malevolent power by… surrendering to it. By yielding to it completely. Suddenly my all-time fa-vorite scene from *Star Wars*—which I have not fully understood until this moment—flashes into my mind: Obi-Wan's lightsaber duel with Darth Vader. As they parry, saber to saber, Darth taunts Obi-Wan: *Your powers are weak, old man.* Obi-Wan responds with a line I have never forgotten: *If you strike me down, I shall become more powerful than you can possibly imagine.* Moments later, as Luke approaches and catches sight of the two locked in combat, Obi-Wan cuts a sidelong glance at him. An almost imperceptible smile plays across his face as he steps back and pulls his lightsaber away from Darth and into a gesture of supplication, of prayer.

As Darth's lightsaber slices savagely through Obi-Wan's now-unprotected body, his robe falls to the floor, utterly empty. *If you strike me down, I shall become more powerful than you can possibly imagine.*

Comprehensions, that had been irretrievable only seconds before, begin to fall towards me like big soft flakes of snow. *Surrender can be more powerful than resistance.* I have just bodily experienced the alchemy of surrender, how a gesture of yielding can transmute even the most oppressive and intractable evil into its own absence. *Blink.* In a bright flash it comes to me that this skill of surrender, of yielding, of not-resisting, of flowing with, has become accessible to me through my movement with the hoop. The hoop, by its nature, will cooperate with your wishes only if you first learn how to follow its inevitable trajectory. The hoop cannot be grabbed and placed where you want it to go: the hoop's own rhythm must first be established, and then—crucially—*listened to.* Baxter often talks about being in *conversation* with the hoop—how, in the best conversations, we move fluidly between talking and listening and back again. The hoop has its own form, its own way, which must be accommodated—which is to say, *felt*—before we can learn how to nudge it towards deeper levels of cooperation. When we try to grab the hoop and force it where we want it to go, we soon find it will either fall, or boomerang back and whap us in the face.

Blink.

A second recognition falls through my post-possession haze: The feeling I have always identified as *fear* is not, in fact, true fear at all, but some radically denatured version of this emotion. What I just *felt* was fear—everything else has been the *resistance to* fear. Real fear is that believing-I'm-going-to-die-at-any-second feeling…a sensation I now know feels genuinely impossible to bear. But I also know now that it can be borne. Any feeling, it occurs to me, might feel unbearable—but this means only that it *feels* unbearable, not that it *is.* And any one of my feelings, I now understand, might be heavily edited, dumbed-down versions of the real deal. It suddenly seems like the strangest of ideas, to avoid the feeling of feelings—when *being felt* is really the only thing they require. And the feeling of my feelings—the purely subjective surrender to them—might be the only way to free myself from their undeniable power over me.

Still another recognition comes my way through the settling dust of this manic episode: *feelings* are not *thoughts*. I now know this because, for the first time in my conscious life, feeling has outpaced thinking. The embodied sensation of fear possessed me *before* my thoughts were able to catch up to it. And I understand, for the first time ever, that feelings are not mental—they are *physical*. Emotion is embodied. I bear my feelings not in my mind, but in my body. What I *think* about my feelings, what I *believe* about them, is something else entirely. And while thoughts and beliefs might have specific influences on the subjective, embodied experience of emotion—and vice versa—they are not one in the same.

Blink.

I do not need to understand my emotions as I'm feeling them, I realize. I can just *feel* them, and *then*—perhaps—come to understand what they might mean (or not mean). I've been so focused on *understanding* my feelings, having them make sense, that I may well have never fully *felt* them. This is the first moment in life where I truly understand that there is an embodied world that exists on its own, apart from the unending skein of *words* that has always served as my primary tool for comprehending this world. Physical reality exists independently, fully, and completely *in addition to* the added layer of language.

The fourth and final revelation that comes to me in these life-altering seconds is a piercing compassion for the overwhelming tendency of the vulnerable human animal to avoid and repress feeling. Because—I now understand—feelings really can be *that bad*. Had I known how close to death I would feel experiencing real fear, would I have chosen to feel it? I have to say (still lying awkwardly halfway off the couch, staring up at the ceiling, unable to move), really, probably not. *Of course* we deny, repress, avoid, evade our feelings. Of course we do. It only seems to make sense to me now, having just discovered that I have spent a lifetime doing (however unconsciously) this very thing.

Blink. Blink.

Bax's face appears above me like a sudden moon. "Baby?!" he says, "What happened?? You've been in here so long!" Over his shoulder, like a rising planet, Kimo's face appears. They both stare down at me with huge dark eyes. I stare back, momentarily mute. "I...I was..." I continue looking at them. Can I explain this extremity of absurdity, that somehow brought me into direct contact with several of the most profound recognitions I've ever experienced? *Emotion is embodied,* I imagine stage-whispering up at them. *Feelings are physical. And all they need is to be felt. And surrender is more powerful than resistance.* I decide I will explain all this a bit later. For now, I just reach my hands up to my brothers, and they pull me back up to my feet.

XII.

Spin

People do not know how what is at variance agrees with itself. It is an attunement of opposite tensions, like that of the bow and the lyre.

— Heraclitus

In order for an object to spin, it must have an axis. An axis is the center line around which the action of spin organizes itself. And a line is an example of a *polarity*: two opposing points that will never, ever meet. Hence, spin depends upon oppositional force, upon irreconcilable difference, upon insurmountable separation.

From the point of view of classical physics—which define the laws that govern what is known as "ordinary" or observable matter—bodies organize themselves through spin. Planets twirl on their axes, revolving around stars, while the stars themselves spin just like our dear Earth, each magic cluster of spinning stars dancing within a huge rotating galaxy, which circles among trillions of observable galaxies…all which seem to be moving within a context—spacetime—of which *curvature* appears to be the single most distinguishing quality.

But there is another point of view in the study of physics—a point of view which would seem to be oppositional, irreconcilable, but which research demands we acknowledge. If we move beyond ordinary matter into a closer scrutiny of subatomic interactions—into the realm known as "quantum"—we find that the distinction between what is matter (a particle) and what is not (a wave) becomes blurred. We have yet to discover a unified theory—a model to which all interactions of all known constituents of reality conform.

In the meantime, among the four forces that are known to organize and regulate the phenomenon we call spacetime, one stands out as less of a force than an immutable property. Its effect is the weakest, but its reach exceeds that of all the other forces. It is called *gravity*, and put simply, it is the fact of spacetime *curvature*.

XIII.

I am taking a long, hot shower in the downstairs bathroom at my mother's house. Tomorrow morning I will get on a plane and fly up to New York to begin my studies. Mary Jean is bringing my dad over shortly, and we are all going to lunch. Over the last two weeks, whenever we go out anywhere, a constant stream of people come up to embrace my father and speak to him. Everyone knows him, and everyone now also knows that—barring some outlandish miracle—he will die soon. I see horror in their eyes. He is a halved version of himself. He has begun radiation and his hair has started to fall out; the trauma of the biopsy has decimated his immense vocabulary. He is still able to ask and answer simple questions, but they are mild, imprecise, hoarse utterances that bear no resemblance to the crisp, musical notes of his true voice. He shuffles weakly across smooth floors, clasping onto Mary Jean to walk even short distances. They will not be coming to the airport tomorrow to see me off.

Over the last two weeks, my life has bustled along urgently. All day every day I prepare for my new life at school, while inside I remain untouched by my father's surreally impending death. I just continue to get ready, seeing friends, choosing clothes, books, posters, buying new toiletries, exchanging cute little cards with my roommate-to-be, Rebecca. There is much too much else to think about; I don't think about my father's sharp decline, it's impossible. But in the brief solitude of the shower, unwanted thoughts and memories bolt to the forefront of my mind.

A conversation with my best friend from several months before replays itself over and over again. One of the many things that unites us is having strained relationships with our fathers. Her immigrant dad hounds her to achieve more and more, never extending his full approval; my father, on the other hand, bombards me with approval and attention, making me feel—now that my brother is off at college—crowded and edgy in ways that I can't understand. One evening, after a particularly bitter session of bitching about our annoying dads, we were holding each other's hands, about to hug goodbye. "But, you know—" she said, her shining eyes looking into mine, "...if my dad *died?* I would feel...so...fucking *horrible*," she gasped, squeezing both my hands tightly. "Oh god..." I replied, my guts sinking under a cold, clammy weight, "—if *my* dad died...that would be the worst—the absolute worst thing that ever happened."

I have never been superstitious—my Christian faith, though muted into an even more pointedly private observance by glimpses of the wider world—remains. But now there is a part of my mind that cannot stop wondering whether by voicing this unthinkable thought—*if my father were to die*—I have somehow brought it into being. Did God hear that conversation? *God hears everything* But that seems ridiculous—even in the depths of my adolescent piety, I don't believe in this kind of direct intervention; I don't believe God sits, like the Fates, ready with scissors to snip the destinies of those who offend. *But why **my** father* I am once again railroaded, by my own thoughts, into the bottomless abyss of my selfishness. *Nothing makes sense* I know it's absurd to imagine that God would do something so petty and punitive, but remembering this conversation brings a terrible, icy guilt. *You shouldn't have said that. You should never, ever have said that.*

The hot water courses over me, washing aside my inexhaustible vigilance. I want nothing more than for all this to disappear, this wrongness that has hijacked my happy, normal, teenage life. And as soon as I catch myself wanting this, I know it is I who am wrong—I am the wrongness at the center of my life, because I cannot make this real, and I cannot feel the way I am supposed to, the way that I *should*. I cannot feel at all. If I do cry, it is in the shower, where the theatrics of my abnormal, unfelt tears cannot be seen or heard.

It was in this shower—an old clawfoot tub surrounded by a jerry-rigging of clear shower curtains and a nozzle dangling by an old coathanger—that I cried alone and stupidly on Christmas afternoon because my father had given me another ring. I had received the first one—a beautiful moonstone in an antique setting—on my 16th birthday. It was pretty but I didn't really want to wear it. What did I want with *rings*? I was a serious student, on my way to a great life of scholarship. I didn't need any *rings*. Once in a while I slipped it on, if I was going to some kind of dress-up event, where skirts and stockings were required.

But then, last Christmas, he presented me with yet another small white box. I felt sick even before opening it to see the artisan-crafted gold band, embedded with a smart rectangle of obsidian. "Thanks, Daddy," I said quickly, clapping the lid back on the box. "I got it at Piedmont Craftsmen," he offered, accelerating past his woundedness with a fact he thought I would like. "It's awesome, thank you," I said evenly, my tone steeled against him, against my capacity to hurt him. *I don't want another ring. I don't want fancy things.* I have intensely disliked my father's pretensions to what I think of as the "jet-set" life: ski trips to Utah, dinner parties in Europe, globetrotting friends with apartments in New York and San Francisco. I have felt personally compromised by what I view as his shallowness. I have never even taken the ring out of the box; I have never put it on my finger.

I hear muffled voices outside the bathroom door. Who's here? Mary Jean is bringing Daddy over at 12:30. It's only about 12:15 right now.

"Annie!" Mom pounds on the door. "Daddy needs to get in there!"

"What?" I sputter through the hot spray. There's another bathroom upstairs. Can he not walk up the *stairs*?

"Daddy needs to get in the bathroom!" she shouts. "Hurry up!"

I haven't conditioned my hair yet, so I quickly spread the smooth glop on my hair, combing it through with my fingers. I have to condition it or it will be weird and tangly.

"Annie, *hurry*!" she yells through the door again.

"I am!" I shout back, rinsing the conditioner out fast, slicking my hands over my head to squeeze out the back of my hair. "I'm almost done!" I can't get out without rinsing my hair!

"*Please!*" she calls, a desperation in her voice that I pretend not to hear.

I get out and dry off quickly. Mom starts opening the door. "Wait!" I shout, grabbing my clothes from the floor, wrapping myself tightly in my long towel.

I step to the door and open it, seeing first my mother, then Mary Jean, then my father, all standing in a line outside the bathroom. Mary Jean lightly holds my father's wrist. The door to the bathroom is wedged behind the sofa, so I have to squeeze past them all, tightly clutching my wad of clothes to my chest. As I pass my father, he looks straight into my eyes, and with a childlike smile, says, "It's...*magic*," spreading his hands as if to indicate a miracle. And that's when I see, on the front of his light blue dress pants, the stain of darkened, wet fabric that is spreading, spreading, over his fly and down his pant legs. "*Magic...*" he says again, with peculiar emphasis, as if he has just begun to believe in it, as Mary Jean takes his elbow and gently begins to guide him, bemused and glassy-eyed, towards the finally-open bathroom door.

* * *

October, 1988

I am home from school for the second time. I flew back last month for my cousin's wedding, in which I was a bridesmaid. The world has not, in fact, stopped in observance of the impossible fact that stands before me at all times like an invisible attendant, whispering urgently: *Your father is dying. Your father is dying.* And though I am aware of this presence at every moment, running beneath everything like groundwater, it cannot become real. It is just sounds, words, information. In my mind, I test it: *My father is dying.* Instinctively I cringe from the shamefulness of forming these words on any level. *You should never have said that.* And yet, inside, I do not feel. Within me there is an exhaustive nothingness, a vast desolation flecked with tiny, buzzing words: *glioblastoma inoperable ganglia father tumor dying.* The words never land anywhere, but just flit around in an amoebic swarm, ungraspable. I watch them, and feel nothing.

The swarm of awareness chases me down the buffed, high-ceilinged hallways of my new university, where I miss not a single orientation event, class, meeting, or advisor appointment. I sit in the front row of every class, my eyes trained steadily on the professor. The tip of my pen never stops moving across the teal-lined pages of my spiral notebook. I fill every page. I write down every word. I will miss nothing—because that is what I am supposed to do, that is what I *want* to do. *You will not stay here, you will not delay your enrollment, you will not interrupt your education for any reason.*

I have to occupy my mind at all times, so that it will not succumb to the swarming awareness as it buzzes on and on: *Your father...your father...* At night, while my peers go across the street to frat parties or downtown to bars, I walk to one of the campus's many libraries to read, study, and complete assignments. If I finish all my work, I go down to the antiquated basement pool to swim laps. I have an unstoppable urge to be *doing things* at all times. *Doing things* means attending class, studying, writing papers, writing letters, reading, exercising, going to the dining hall (my sole social activity) with my roommate and our new bffs, Jess and Sarah. *Doing things* does not mean going to parties, going out to bars, joining groups, dancing, meeting guys, going to games, or behaving in any way like typical college students who spend four years drunk, wasting their parents' money.

I'm home just for the weekend, so as not to miss any classes. Daddy has moved in with Mary Jean and her two young children. The house is small, tidy, and cozy. My father stays in the downstairs bedroom, in a rented hospital bed. For reasons I don't fully understand, they have continued radiation, so his hair is gone. A few baby-bird tufts remain, clinging awkwardly to his skull. He takes steroids, too, so his face is always red and swollen into an odd, eggplanty shape. His solid, energized body has dwindled to a slack, spindly working of bones with a distended belly. No longer in control of his bladder, he has to wear a catheter at all times. Since I was last home, just a month ago, he has lost entirely the abilities to both walk and talk.

On Saturday morning, I drive over to Mary Jean's. She suggests I take my father for a drive—he hasn't been out in a while. We get him in the rented wheelchair and roll him, bundled in pajamas, socks, slippers, robe, long wool coat and scarf, up to the passenger door of the Volkswagen he bought for me last year. It takes us several minutes to trundle him in. I reach over him to grab his seat belt and click it into place. Mary Jean and the kids wave to us as I back slowly out of the driveway and begin our drive through the lightly overcast, lovely fall day.

I do not speak to my father. It seems too awful that he cannot speak back. The placement and size of the tumor, the doctors have said, affect not only the language centers of my father's brain, but also his capacity to feel emotion. The last time my mother spoke to him, weeks ago when he could still talk, he said to her: "It's not happy, it's not sad, it's just—" and then he raised his hand and moved his flat palm in a straight, horizontal line.

I drive down Mary Jean's short block to a stop sign at the busy main road. I don't know where my father would want to go. Should we turn left, to go out to the country? Or right, towards town? I look over at my dad. His expression is blank, his eyes almost beadily fixed ahead. To my shock, he raises one arm straight out in front, palm extended, and pushes it *right*. So we go *right*, towards town.

We drive down the main thoroughfare to the five-point intersection where his law firm's squat, tan, 60s-era building is located. My father loves his job and has always spent extra hours at the office, sometimes taking my brother and me for an hour or so on the evenings we would spend the night with him. When we were younger, it was a thrill to run around the empty carpeted hallways, peering into the vacant offices and feeling the weirdness of the dark windows against the fluorescent overhead light. Greg and I would play with the Xerox machine, copying our mashed faces, hands, and feet while Daddy moved papers mysteriously around on his desk and marked notes on long yellow pads in his tight, wavy script.

His office was where he had taken me to issue another of his rare parental decrees. I was in the eighth grade—the height of my budding juvenile delinquency—and had just been caught skipping school with a few of my rebel friends. We were sneaking cigarettes and swigs of my dad's seldom-touched supply of hard liquor (we went to my dad's house, of course, because it was within walking distance of the school, and never locked). Earlier in the year I had also been caught bragging on the phone about sneaking out at the beach, walking down to a local Ramada Inn, and hanging out and drinking with a group of Marines.

One evening several days after the school-skipping incident, after Daddy had taken me out for dinner (my brother was absent for some reason), he said, with a studied casualness, "Come up to the office for a minute with me, Annie." I knew something dire was in the air. Would I be grounded? Would I be barred forever from going to the mall?? What was he going to say?? Cold dread crept into me.

We walked through the silent hallways to his ample, neatly appointed office. On the open shelf right behind his desk were large framed photographs of myself and my brother. My father guided me around to his side of the desk, pointed to his large swivel office chair, and told me to sit down. He then walked back around the desk to sit opposite me, in one of the black wooden West Point chairs where guests and clients sat. His face was calm, his elbows perched on the high armrests of the uncomfortable chair, hands pressed fingertip to fingertip in front of his chin. He glanced briefly out into the placid night, then turned his clear eyes back to me.

"Annie," he began, "Let me tell you something. *You*...are on a *path*." I focused all my attention on maintaining eye contact. "And when you get to the *end* of that path"—he moved his hands apart, making a closed loop of one thumb and forefinger, which he then pointed right at me, his blue eyes unwavering—"what you are going to *find*, is a bag full of *shit*." My mind exploded in shock—my father had never before spoken the word *shit* in my presence, nor had I ever overheard him say it to anyone else. I was 14 years old. Within a few months I would be completing my first week at the all-girls' school, murmuring my mantra of unparalleled happiness as I—seemingly without effort—transformed into exactly the person I now knew my father wanted me to be.

The light turns green and my father's arm shoots out again, this time swinging *left*. We turn onto the wide, lush avenue that bisects the double row of grand stucco mansions built with tobacco money. Massive oaks line both sides of the street, their changing leaves appearing nowhere on the huge, immaculate green lawns in front of every house. The car sweeps along, full of silence and the whisper of my new tires on the smooth black asphalt. In my father's car, the radio is always on: NPR, Casey Kasem's top 40, or oldies. We always sing along noisily. At home, his Gibson acoustic never rests in its case, but sits perpetually propped against the couch, where he can pick it up at any moment to figure out a tune or start up a family singalong. If there is any kind of gathering, he is sure to bring the guitar, and keep singing until the party is over. I am jolted by the sudden realization that I cannot remember the last time I heard him sing.

Right. We turn down the shady, median-split street where our old house stands, where the four of us once lived together as a family. I hardly remember my parents together...we saw much less of my dad when he actually lived with us. He was home in the evenings for dinner and to kiss us good-night; on the weekends he would mow the yard, wearing a clamshell face mask to keep out the pollen. When he was done he would join us in the backyard to play touch football. One Saturday, when I was about four, Mom decided she wanted to do some shopping, and told Greg and me we were going to stay home with Daddy. I was rocked with a piercing unease—we never stayed home alone with Daddy! Somehow it seemed he would not know what to do, how to take care of us. So during the shuffle as she was getting ready to walk out the door, I sneaked out to her yellow VW squareback and lay down on the smooth brown hooked weave of the cargo hatch. I stayed completely still and silent as she drove to the fabric store, popping up to watch her disappear inside. I scrambled out and followed, staying a good 15 feet behind her as she perused the aisles, her mouth and eyes flying open when she finally turned to see me trudging doggedly in her wake. "Annie!" she cried, in amused dismay. She took my hand and rushed to the counter so she could borrow their phone and call my father. The memory, once funny, now sickens me. *He knew I didn't love him. He must have known, even then.*

Right. Past the vast, rolling grounds of the Children's Home, where no children ever run. Past the snarled overgrowth by the creek that runs up to the old train track. Under the concrete trestle, marbled with puffy graffiti tags. Behind the huge old public high school, where I would have gone if my parents hadn't forced me to go to the girls' school. For the first time it hits me that, had they not done that, there is *no way* I would be living in New York right now. My breath stops for a moment as I contemplate where—had I been permitted to continue my tear of delinquency—I might be right now. Past the wide, open park with the tennis courts where I would sneak smokes every day with my bad-kid friends in middle school. Past the frozen yogurt parlor, where I would park at night in 10th grade to spy on my ex-boyfriend while he worked inside. Past the consignment shop, past the paint store with the rainbow insignia, past the strange dun-colored rectangular pest control building, and up the long hill, up to where my father's three-story restored Victorian house stands.

Ten years ago the house was to be demolished by a local radio station looking to build a parking lot. My dad got wind of it somehow and pursued a deal, ultimately buying the house for $1 and then moving it—on two fat red trucks—a couple of blocks away, onto an elevated lot that proved almost disastrous after a soaking rain. But the house managed to make the journey in one piece. My dad converted (meaning: paid for the conversion of) the two upper floors into apartments, each with a spiral staircase. The house is painted a deep gray with pink and white trim-work—a San Franciscoish look he dearly wanted. It is beautiful.

Left. We pull slowly, slowly up to the house. I parallel park at the curb, even though we always pull up the winding driveway to park in back. Is this still my father's home? What does that even mean? We couldn't go inside anyway; we would need the wheelchair. I can't bear to think about this. From inside the car, my father and I peer up at the house like tourists. The yard is trim and kempt; there are no piles of newspapers or stacks of accumulated mail on the porch—my father's friend of many years, John, has taken over managing all his daily affairs and obligations. Renters still live in both upstairs apartments. The downstairs consists of four large rooms, a wide central hallway, narrow bathroom, and tiny, nearly unused kitchen. The two front rooms doubled as bedrooms for me and Greg when we would stay with him—each couch folded out into a bed; we kept our pillows and comforters on shelves tucked behind. When he got out of the shower in the mornings (having awakened at or before 5:30 a.m., an old Army habit), Daddy would wrap himself in his long gray towel to come wake each of us up, tiny droplets falling from his damp hair as he kissed our noses.

After a minute, my father's fixed, glacial gaze slides back towards the windshield. And again he raises his arm, pointing our direction with his whole hand, his whole arm. *Forward.*

XIV.

February 13th, 1989

It is early evening. I am alone in my dorm room in New York; my roommate having gone, as she often does, to a ballet class. The tan, sleek, Jet-
sons-style phone—room phones are new to the dorms as of this year—
begins to ring. I know it must be my mother. I pick up the receiver and
bring it to my ear.

"Hello?"

"Annie," she says. I hear her breathing, as though she has just climbed
flights of stairs. She does not—as she always does—immediately lob
a question at me about a paper or class assignment, the topics we stay
welded to in most of these conversations. Right before we hang up, she
will provide a quick, factual update on my father's condition, from which
we can both easily escape.

"It's me—" I reply. I am aware of the space she has left open, but I do
not dare to fill it with a question.

"Well," she begins, her voice swinging up and down wildly, "he's
gone…" And her voice breaks into a sob.

For one second, a searing fury possesses me. "Do you mean he's
dead?" I snap viciously, outraged at being forced to speak out the explicit
truth, in words, in my voice. This rage is the only clear feeling. Tears
muddle my vision, but inside I am so cold and hard and far away. We
hang up quickly, and I dial the airline to book the next flight home.

A few hours later, I am one of only a handful of people on a late-night flight from LaGuardia to Greensboro. I have packed my red duffel and thrown it into the overhead bin. I sit in one of the back rows, next to the window. The most important thing I hold in my lap: my black and silver Walkman, which plays a cassette tape of my father's favorite album, Jimmy Buffett's *Songs You Know by Heart*.

> *Mother, mother ocean*
> *I have heard you call*
> *Wanted to sail upon your waters*
> *Since I was three feet tall—*
> *You've seen it all,*
> *You've seen it all—*

I see my dim reflection in the tiny plastic oval of the airplane window—the whitish face, hollowed eyes, thin wrists poking out of the dull gray sweatshirt. The front of the sweatshirt is clotted with dark blotches from my tears, which fall with a disturbing randomness. I squeeze my eyes shut tightly, then open them again. *This isn't real.*

There is only one flight attendant in the coach section tonight. She walks by silently, her red-nailed hands brushing the empty seatbacks; she can tell something is wrong, something has happened to me. I don't want to have to say it again, so every time she passes, asking gently if there's anything I need, I smile the irreproachable smile of the well-to-do Southern female, which denies everything and allows nothing. "No, thank you, I'm fine." She leans close, wanting to hug me—I know she feels terrible for me, she is so quiet and kind. Even as tears course down my face, I smile my polite, deflecting smile. I have learned how to keep people away if I want to.

> *Yes, I am a pirate*
> *Two hundred years too late*
> *The cannon don't thunder there's nothing to plunder*
> *I'm an over-forty victim of fate—*

Arriving too late,
Arriving too late—

My father was fifty. My father *was*?! No. *Fifty years old. You are nineteen.* He was only fifty. He was thirty-one when I was born; both my parents were. When I was born I might have died, I was a breech birth and they couldn't turn me and I couldn't be born and inhaled meconium and could have suffocated, but I didn't. They told my parents, *If her heart is strong enough, she will make it. If her lungs are strong enough. There is nothing else we can do.* For two days I lay in an incubator in the preemie unit, a huge, unnaturally white baby gasping for oxygen amidst the sea of tiny red and brown newborns. My mother told me that my father, after every sentence the doctors spoke, could only repeat, *But she's going to be all right, isn't she? But she's going to be all right, isn't she?*

The plane drifts through the limitless black night. Up in the sky, I am utterly alone, cushioned by emptiness. Below me, I see constellations of light—evidence of humanity scattered across the dark and fluctuating topography. How impossible to be up here. I've flown plenty of times—once to Europe—but this is the first time I have felt so aware of the sky's radical emptiness. I am surrounded by...nothing: there is nothing under me, nothing above me, nothing to either side. Nothing. There's nothing anywhere.

Like a silent, terrible crack of lightning, the idea of God splits through all my other thoughts. *What have I been thinking about??* I haven't thought about God in...I don't know, when did I last think of God? *Is God out there? Right now? In all that emptiness?* Cold fear sweeps through me for a second *God sees everything, God knows* but in the next second, I look across the aisle, out the other plastic airplane window, exactly like my own *there's emptiness on all sides* and, as I stare through the small black oval, I am suddenly revolted to think of my father's soul.

Because I haven't thought once about his soul, I haven't thought about him having a soul, I haven't thought about—not even once, not even for a second—what might happen to it. *How dare they, how dare they make me think* Because my father is not a Christian, it hasn't made sense to think about, I don't believe in heaven and hell anyway *but where did he go?* I don't even believe in that fire-and-brimstone crap, the true God would never judge, but still there is this unbearable thought in my mind, because I don't know where my father *went,* I realize I don't know where he *is* now *he didn't "go" anywhere, he's just dead* But they would say, they would say he is in hell, he rejected Christ, my father rejected the authority of Christ *my father is not in hell* How could they…how could anyone think…my father *my father is not in hell* just because he didn't *believe??!* And the whole idea that someone has a *soul* that could be *condemned?!!* To some fucking *place* that no one has even *seen??!!?*

Because I suddenly know, above and beyond everything else that I have ever known, or believed about anything, from any source, from any authority, with an indomitable certainty I now know—above all conceivable things in this world, and any world beyond—that

my   father   is   not   in   hell

And because I know this, I know now there is no hell, and I know now there can be no God, either.

* * *

The flight attendant rolls her cart by again. I keep my eyes pointed down, at the tiny whirling wheels inside the gray box of my Walkman, because only they now can connect me to my father who has disappeared into nothingness without telling me where he would be, or how I might find him.

As a dreamer of dreams and a travelin man
I have chalked up many a mile—
Read dozens of books about heroes and crooks
And learned much from both of their styles—

What did he believe? Why do I not know this? *You never knew him. And now you can't.* I recall abruptly how he used to say to my brother and me: "I really look forward to being your friend one day." I had no idea what he was talking about. He would tell us, "When you all grow up, you can call me 'Jim.'" I would swat his shoulder and shout, "I'm *never* going to call you 'Jim'!! I'm only ever calling you *Daddy!!*" He would cackle, tickling me and saying, "Noooo, I want you to call me *Jim!*" and I would scream: "*NO!!! I'm never, ever calling you 'Jim'! You're Daddy!!*"

We inhabit only one universe, and my father has disappeared into it…through it…beyond it. *And where is that??* These questions have never appeared to me before, because I was so sure, I was so certain that God (*who??????*) was in the driver's seat, wearing a seat belt, having clicked mine into place long ago. And I was so certain (*why?????*) that no one would be left behind. *You didn't think of him. You never thought of him.*

The unbearable truth that is dawning is that I have never really *thought* about anything, at all. If I had, I would have seen that all human creatures inhabit and share a single universe, and that any and all claims to know the will of "God" are sheer fabrications, built on a foundation of absolute nothingness. I would have seen the obviousness of the fact that, throughout the millennia of human history, no one correctly-believing religious group has been specially chosen for salvation. I would have seen the ugliness of a judgment designed to exclude my two closest friends—one Hindu, the other Unitarian—from this purported salvation. I would have seen the nauseating spectacle of my own hypocrisy, as I selected the new clothes and slept in the beautiful safe homes and read the mountain of books and drove the nice European car and wolfed down the good food that were all paid for with my once-Christian father's money.

> *And all of the answers and all of the questions*
> *Locked in his attic one day—*
> *Cause he liked the quiet, clean country living*
> *And twenty more years slipped away*

* * *

As I float, minute by minute, through this new emptiness, through the indelible consequence of my failure to comprehend even the simplest, most self-evident thing—that we inhabit only one universe—unwanted realizations continue to pierce like shrapnel through my relentless consciousness. I cannot stop the assault of these conclusions as they descend in swarms from some terrible and hidden place.

I don't know that I know anything. Now that I have understood the audacity of my assumption that God was in his heaven (*and why would God be male???*) and all was right with the world, I can't stop the flow of recognizing—in a single, stomach-turning wave—the sheer volume of everything I have failed to take into account in my vision of reality. *I don't even know what the universe is.*

I have never felt the slightest inclination to study physics, astronomy, higher math (or math at all), space, time. I haven't the dimmest idea how space and time are connected, are part of a continuum, although many seem to understand that they are. I've never been interested in numbers, or in any math beyond fractions, ratio, and proportion. I haven't the vaguest concept of what constitutes a "dimension," but this idea has become—in an instant—direly significant. *Where did he go? Where is he now?* Mine are the thoughts of a kindergartner, a foolish and insufficiently curious child.

Suddenly, an even worse thought raises itself out of this morass and stabs me in the face. It is so much more awful than any of the other thoughts, because it exposes to me—definitively and indisputably—the hideous and intractable depth of my narcissism. The thought that comes out of nowhere is: *No one believes in me.*

My father, from the moment of my birth (*but she's going to be all right, isn't she?*) has believed—generously, constantly, without reservation—in my uniqueness, my inevitable destiny, my capacity to do anything, do everything. My father has believed me to be a certain person—an exceptional person, big-hearted, smart and fair, a person with talents and gifts and clear responsibilities to the world—and I have believed myself to be this person, too. Now, with a sickening sensation of falling, my reliance on his vision of me as my vision of myself delineates itself sharply from the morass. *I might not be a good person. I might not even be that smart.*

Just as instantly, I am drowning in a thick slime of shame at the extremity of my self-obsession. I have been proud of my abilities to see outside my perspective; I have thought of myself as broad-minded, well-read, generous in my own right, mature for my age, able to take in the widest possible range of truths. Suddenly, my own thoughts—which can't be attributed to anyone but me inside this empty, drifting plane—can't not force me into recognizing my own monstrousness. *No one believes in me anymore.*

I am nothing
I am no one
I do not exist

* * *

The flight bores on through the newly-vacant night sky. All that is unthinkable and unbearable continues to synthesize into newly-comprehensible thoughts whose self-evidence and clarity refuse reproach. The authority of my mind, which has been able to sensibly narrate so much of my brief life, no longer has any kind of managing role—thoughts leer from unimagined corners, unexamined truths popping out of the empty depths surrounding me, the fragile mirrors of my entirely illusory teenage self shattering all at once, without making a sound.

Amidst this assault of thought, tears continue to slip down, interrupting my thoughts with their cold strangeness. And within me, beneath the racing thoughts that rivet my attention without mercy, is the hard, cold tundra of my heart, which—still—will not feel what is happening, what I *know* to be happening. Like a hard slap, the most frightening thought of all hits me without warning: *I do not believe that he is dead.*

I force my mind towards this fact, which nothing in the universe can change now: *he is dead he is is dead you know he is dead.* But, terrifyingly, the more I push push push my mind to engulf this reality—which is something I must do; it is a new requirement of the universe I now inhabit, a universe in which he no longer exists—the more it swerves devilishly away. *You watched him dying,* the part of me that is still rational insists. *You saw him waste away.* His devastated body, empty eyes, slack and silent mouth. I force my mind towards these horrors, because in order to stay sane I have to make myself believe, I have to understand that *he is dead* now, he has disappeared from being—where his warm and singly familiar body was, where his huge mind was housed, where his blue eyes sparkled with the irrepressible joy of being, there is now *nothing, nothing,* do you understand?!! *There is nothing where he was, and nothing will ever be there again. Where he was, there is nothing now. He is dead and so he doesn't exist.*

But somehow the more I point my mind towards this incontestable fact—the only fact that could now possibly matter—the more I find the simple and terrifyingly irrational belief that he will be in his house when I return…he will be at Mary Jean's…he will be seated behind his desk at the office, his pen poised sharply above one of many legal pads. *He will **be** somewhere…*some deepest part of me commands, from beyond thought or language—from beyond reason itself.

I think of Winston-Salem, of all the buildings and homes and restaurants where he might want to be, and still he inhabits them, somehow. He is not gone. *He is DEAD* my rational mind insists helplessly. I still feel him to be at home; when I look for him, there is not emptiness—he is there. *He's dead he's dead you know he's dead—so you're insane, you know you're insane.* If I'm not sane, then I can't go back to school, and finish my semester with the highest GPA I have ever achieved. *You will not stay here, you will not delay your enrollment, you will not interrupt your education for any reason.*

I *must* not not be sane. I cannot lose my mind. I must *not* succumb to this; I must force myself to believe the reality that cannot be refuted. *My father is dead.* I will not fall apart like a crazy person and waste the lifetime of resources he so carefully cultivated for me. *No.* I will *not* dishonor him, I will *not* disappoint him. I will *make* myself believe.

I will make myself believe this worst thing imaginable. It has happened and I will believe it; I *will. My father is dead* and nothing can be done; no one can do anything. I thought he could do anything. *He held up the world* and now there is nothing; there is only me with my fragment of reason. Therefore, I will believe in his death; I will *make* myself believe it somehow. And I will not look back, and I will not fall apart, and I will not be crazy.

I   will

not

be

crazy.

* * *

It has been six weeks since I turned 19. Over the next seven days, I will design and plan every detail of my father's funeral. I will choose his burial urn, marker, and plot—overruling my beloved grandmother who wants him to be buried in the hometown he hated, near her. I will evaluate every object in his home, and select what is to be kept and what will be folded and placed into brown packing boxes or bagged up in enormous black trash bags to be taken without ceremony to Goodwill. I will make every single one of these judgments alone, with no help or input. There is no one else who can make them, and my brother would rather trust my judgment than take part in these agonizing decisions himself. *It's up to you,* my big brother says to me, again and again and again. *It's up to you.*

On the evening of the seventh day, I will fly back up to New York. The next morning I will be the first one to arrive at my African-American Lit class; as always, I will sit on the front row, directly in front of the professor, where I can be sure to take in every single word that he says.

For the remainder of my time at school—three and a half more years—I will not miss another class.

XV.

Space/Time

For someone to be able to live she must either not see the infinite, or have such an explanation of the meaning of life as will connect the finite with the infinite.

— Leo Tolstoy

The day my father died, I was cut adrift in a newly infinite universe—a place far too vast, immeasurable, and complicated ever to be grasped. This was a circumstance I had never given a moment's thought to: I had considered myself to exist safely in the palm of a disembodied—yet somehow categorically male—entity named "God."

The absurdity of the idea that "God" spoke in only one way through a single person just two thousand years ago—when humanity had already existed for millennia—broke over me in an irreversible tsunami. I was now underwater, never again to breathe the rarefied air of unexamined belief.

But I was still a creature who needed air to live.

* * *

Knowledge—if I am honest with myself, an end towards which I doggedly strive—is itself a kind of faith. How do we know what we know? In the hours following my dad's death, it became crucial to verify what tiny fund of knowledge remained for me in this newly-empty, newly-impossible phenomenon—the universe—of which I was incontestably a part.

In the selfsame moment, it became clear to me what a slippery and uncertain slope this verification process could be. *How do we know what we know?*

The foundation I had vaguely and osmotically internalized—that there was a male entity somewhere, paying attention and keeping score and intervening when necessary to ensure that everyone was recognizing the right things in this life—disappeared without a trace. I needed a new foundation, one that would never disappear into nothingness without warning. I needed a foundation based on the kinds of truths that were testable and verifiable by science; however, having almost no grounding in the hard sciences, I just did not know what these foundations were.

I needed a *metaphor*—a symbol that could cut across chasms of understanding too immense for language and numbers to bridge. I needed a *shape* that could speak to me about the nature and organization of matter and energy, the way that *what we know* (because we *do* know a little something) locates itself within perceptible forms and patterns which—when taken together—do make some kind of gloriously improbable *sense*.

I needed something…something…that could speak to me in shorthand about this universe we have all so implausibly been born into, something that could inform me about everything that surrounded me, everything that continues and continues to flow on so irrevocably, and my place within all that everythingness. I needed a way to understand the universe—a way that did not involve some intervening unseeable unfathomable imaginary dude.

I just could not envision what such a thing might be.

XVI.

...Who knows?
perhaps the same bird echoed through both of us
yesterday, separate, in the evening...

— Rainer Maria Rilke

July, 2007

Kimo and I are hooping under the breezeway at the park down the street from the co-op. A summer rain falls softly on the tin roof. The wet air is warm. Clouded gray light shines down through the skylights and shimmers across Kimo's shiny blue-green-silver hoop, which he has nicknamed "Bluebird." It is late afternoon; no one else is around.

For the last year, he and I have been hooping two hours a day, with Baxter in his backyard. We have honed our meager hoop skills to the point where we can dance more or less freely, without having to think ahead and plan out every move. The simple bliss of having a reason and a way to dance every day is astounding.

Kimo still mostly practices his own methods of hooping; he does some of the moves I've learned going to Baxter's class every week, but a lot of what he does in the hoop comes from his own experimental process (which he Canadianly pronounces "*PROE-cess*," to Baxter's and my unending merriment). While I have carefully copied Bax's hoop-filming techniques: setting up on my patch in the backyard, filming unplanned flow sequences, then capturing the best three or four minutes to post—Kimo has set up his own shots in his studio, hanging a stark white backdrop for contrast, choosing a spare Tuvan throat-singing track to set off his unusual, slow-mo moves with the hoop. We have all been posting our progress (*PROE-gress*) on the newly popular video-sharing site, YouTube.

Because of this, and because of our hoop-based social networking hub—a community-run site started through the Burning Man festival—over the last year we have "met" several hoopers across the globe. Even though we have never danced together in person (although Bax has met a few of them at previous burns), these hoopfriends feel like a second family. And tomorrow—after four frenetic months of planning—18 of these hoopers will be flying here to North Carolina to join us for a long weekend of hoopship. We are going to have workshops and potlucks and jams and over 72 hours of nonstop hoop geekery. We have worked out everything to the last tiny detail.

Except, tomorrow—when the hoopers start to arrive in the early afternoon—Kimo will not be with us. He will be anesthetized and laid out flat on an operating table, where doctors will be cutting open his head for the third time.

We found out just 48 hours ago that his latest scan was not clear. He had been going in for regular scans every three months since his last recurrence two years ago. He walked slowly across the front lawn of the co-op and plopped down at one of the green picnic tables with me and Baxter, where we were downing a quick lunch. At first, he didn't mention it.

But the weird look on his face caused me to press him: "What's going on, Hon?"

"I just had a scan..." he said heavily. He had *just* had a clear one.

"Oh," I said, automatically tamping down a swell of panic. "What did they say?"

"It's growing again—" he groaned. "I have to go in for surgery on *Thurs*day." More than anything, he was angry about missing the hoopers. "I wanted to meet everybody!" he cried, the anguish hiding in the back of his voice.

"You *will*," I said steadily. I would take everyone to meet him. They had to meet him! Goddamn fucking tumor! I didn't cry until Baxter and I were walking away from him, back to the car, where he couldn't see my face.

* * *

Kimo has brought along his new playlist—a compilation of underground hip-hop from New Orleans—and is singing along loudly to Kane & Abel as he swings Bluebird around his core: "*I know you got a maaaaaaaan, but I don't caaa—aaaa—aaaare....*" He throws his head back as he sings, lifting his arms into funkified Two Bird formations. Lifeforce ripples through him. We dance over the smooth concrete, swinging our bodies to the deep and dirty beats as the rain murmurs everywhere around us.

"Ah, god dammit!" Kimo bursts out in a pause between songs. "I can't believe I won't get to meet all the hoopers!" He passes Bluebird from hand to hand, around the equator of his waist. He wants to spend as much time as he possibly can hooping and making art before the surgery tomorrow.

"I'm gonna bring some people to the hospital, K," I quickly reassure him. "Some hot babes," I say with a wink.

"This fucking tumor!" he shouts into the warm misty air. He looks strikingly healthy with his summer tan and chiseled frame from the hours and hours and hours of dancing we've shared. A new song starts up, and he throws the hoop around his waist, bending his knees low to create an angle. It is simply not conceivable that tomorrow a saw will be buzzing through his skull, little tiny microscalpels scraping through the precious matter of his brain.

His ex-girlfriend Laena will be arriving tonight to accompany him to the surgery tomorrow morning. When he last had the tumor resection, two years ago, there were complications: the irradiated square of skin over the original incision site—which was also the second and will be the third incision site—at first refused to heal. After bouncing out of the hospital only a couple days post-surgery, Kimo immediately had to go back in for two consecutive lumbar drains—meaning, huge needles installed for five days into his lower back to drain the pressure of his spinal fluid on the stapled-up incision site. The second one worked: his incision stopped leaking spinal fluid, his skin began to knit back together, and he went home and right back to work. Laena will be here for two weeks this time. If he sustains further complications, I will be his primary support.

Without us having to discuss it, we both understand that this is so. His family members cannot suddenly drop their lives thousands of miles away to come and care for him—his aunt and mother are elderly, not American citizens, and don't have the resources to make such a move. His younger brothers are embedded in their lives in Western Canada. And Kimo is healthier now than I have ever seen him; energetic and strong, he has never looked better. He's smoking a lot less and making eye-popping artwork with large photo transfers and tobacco-treated paper. It's implausible that he would have any more complications than he had last time.

"Annie," he lets the hoop hang in his hand as he swivels his head towards me, his face suddenly slack, blank. "I'm really scared this time."

My heart blooms with dread, which I glide over instinctively. "I know it, sweetie." My voice is steady. My task is to remain in a place of clarity and reason, to help him marshal all the resources necessary for his healing. Kimo praises me on a regular basis for being "sane." I know—without his having to tell me—that this is the quality he most needs me to embody as he faces all this down yet again. He can feel my unflinchingness; unlike most friends, who become self-conscious and awkward when the conversation turns to brain cancer, I am always prepared to discuss it in detail—without ever breaking eye contact.

"There's more risk..." he begins. I know what he wants to say. Every time they scrape tumor cells out of his right parietal lobe, there is a risk of not only the irradiated skin failing to heal, but also paralysis on the left side of his body. We have never talked about this specifically terrifying chance, but I've known about it since his last surgery.

"I know," I say firmly. I want him to know I understand, he doesn't have to explain. I want him to feel the continuity I fully expect in our lives—how we will flow from this moment through the surgery and onto more art, more dancing and exploring...we have already started planning our outfits for our first burn with Baxter in August. Kimo has been drawing sketches of himself in heroic, flowing hoopgear—all to be sewn out of repurposed clothing. For him, absolutely everything is an art project.

"I just fucking hate the hospital," he says, a bitterness sharpening his voice as he gazes down at the concrete beneath us. "I hate it so much."

"It fucking sucks," I concur grimly, remembering the weird space-age vibe of the premier research hospital just a mile and a half from where we are standing: the purple-white of fluorescent light ricocheting off the slick floor tiles, the awful tang of electric currents permeating the air like offgas. The alternating nosefuls of medical-grade disinfectant with the yeasty funk of aging bodies, the occasional swell of leftover applesauce. Kimo doesn't belong there.

"I feel so strong right now. I feel stronger than ever."

"You are."

Standing in front of me in his soft blue t-shirt and long gray shorts, shiny black hair pulled back into a thick ponytail, bouncing from one foot to the other like a stoked teenager, Kimo is the picture of health and verve. A light sweat stands out on his oaky skin; his deep brown eyes shine with anxious curiosity. To see him is to believe that he will rocket straight back into this robust body post-surgery...he might even, I daydream, be able to join us at the Hoopers' Ball on Sunday night—wouldn't that be just perfect?

Kimo glances over his shoulder to where his old white Honda is parked. "I think I gotta go pick up Laena—" he realizes, walking over to his pile of stuff to check his cell phone. She will stay with him tonight, waking up with him at 4 a.m. to drive to the hospital. Behind all my thoughts there is the white wall of panic—a whistling emptiness that contains all unthinkable possibilities, which I do not admit into the realm of thought.

"Okay, Honey. I will see you tomorrow. I'll be there as soon as Laena calls." I hug him close. He smells like fresh paint and sweat and cigarettes and him.

"Okay, Annie! We'll see ya!" The powerful beam of his smile, for a moment, eases everything—his voice never too many notes away from wonder, or joy.

* * *

The next afternoon, after the first wave of hugging and hooping and happy shouts of greeting have subsided, I jump in my car and—leaving the hoopers at the same spot under the breezeway where Kimo and I just danced beneath the rain—zap to the hospital. I park in the enormous parking deck and scuttle across the walkway to the tightly packed cluster of huge, indistinguishable hospital buildings.

I find my way to the "step-down" unit, where patients are taken for the first few hours after surgery, while the strong anesthetic wears off. Laena sprints to the open door to meet me, pulling me back out into the hallway. I have a split-second sighting of Kimo, smiling from beneath a tangle of white PICC lines. "Annie!" he calls, sounding ecstatic. "Hey, Honey!" I shout back. "One second!" He looks like he is trying to raise his arm.

Laena doesn't speak at first, but stares at me, big tears standing in her eyes. Her lips press together urgently. "He's still coming off painkillers—" she reports, with a sharp inhale.

"Annie! Oh my gawd…you *gotta* check it out…" Kimo burbles blissfully from just inside the door.

"How is he?" I hold Laena's gaze.

She inhales audibly again. "The left side—" She squeezes her eyes shut, tears spilling out.

"He can't move?" *Just yesterday we were dancing…dancing beneath the rain…*

Laena keeps her eyes closed as she shakes her head *No,* shaking the tears that hang at her jawline.

"*Annie!*" Kimo shouts in delirious joy.

"He's still so high, I don't know if he can tell—" whispers Laena.

I nod and squeeze her hand as we walk back into the unit.

"Annie!!" Kimo exclaims from his nest of white wires. He is wearing a baby blue hospital gown and swaddled in a thin white blanket. He looks radically shrunken, his head wrapped in a huge puffy bandage—but his smile is positively beatific. "These people are AMAZING!" he gushes. "These doctors, they're just wonderful," he says, seeming to struggle to sit up. The nurse stationed next to his bed gently reminds him he has to lie down.

"Oh…*sorey,*" he says with Canadian politesse, looking up at her like a grateful child at his teacher. I move closer to the bed to bend down and kiss him. Only his right arm reaches back.

"How are you, Honey?" I ask, holding tight to his perfect right hand.

"Oh, I'm *great*," he says fervently. "The people here are just *incredible*." He glances around at the nurse, Laena, me. "I can't believe how amazing these people are."

"But Annie! Check it out—" he says, suddenly looking down at his motionless left arm. "I can make"—his blissed-out smile breaking forth again— "a PEACE sign!" From underneath the web of white PICC lines, his limp left hand begins to rise, listing slowly from side to side, as though it cannot balance. "...peace sign..." he says, studying his swaying hand with the concentration of a child learning to write.

Laena catches my eye from across the bed. Her eyes still leak tears, her mouth pressed into a bizarrely encouraging grin. We can't tell him now. When will he realize...?

"...*peace sign*..." Kimo insists, still beaming, still focused on his weirdly clawed left hand as it pitches from side to side. "Just a...second..." he says, his belief in the force of his will undiminished.

Inside the hard clarity I have wordlessly pledged to maintain for him, I remain motionless. *I will bear witness, I will not look away, I will not lie.* This isn't really a lie, it's just a moment that he can't do without—I won't rob him of the joy of coming back to life after having his skull opened and scraped out. My feelings are frozen in a chasm between the possible—*He's okay, he made it*—and the impossible—*He can't walk anymore, he can't dance.*

Laena and I continue to watch him try to lift his weakly swaying arm, looking at him rather than each other.

Just yesterday we were dancing, dancing under the rain

* * *

Kimowan's mother was only seventeen when he was born. His father was a Canadian soldier whom he never met; I don't think he ever knew of Kimo's existence. His stepfather was an unhinged and sadistic white man who terrorized him and his mother. Once, when we were looking through old family photos, we found her adorable high school picture from the early 60s—wearing granny glasses and a peter pan collar with her pageboy haircut and bright pink lipstick. When I flipped the photo over, I saw the words written in disturbingly jagged blue ballpoint: *She was whoring even then.*

When Kimo was twelve years old, his mother shook him awake in the middle of the night. "I'm leaving," she whispered. "You can come with me if you want." They lay on the floorboards of a friend's truck for the next fifteen hours. Eleven years passed before he saw his three younger brothers again.

In the Cree language, there are many different words for *rain.* The word *kimowan* means *a fine, light, steady rain*—the kind of rain that surrounds the whole heart with its quiet song.

* * *

September, 2007

I check in at the visitor station and start running up to Kimo's room. It's late—close to midnight. The hospital hallways are nearly empty. I was here in the afternoon to bring him some pasta; I left around dinnertime. Then, about 20 minutes ago, he called my cell phone, his voice weirdly indistinct.

"Anneh—ehheh—eheh—" he coughed, his throat clouded. "Itsch…itsch…not good," he burbled.

"What's going on? What's happening?"

"Itscha…aahh…aahhh…*seizure…*"

"You're having a seizure?" Kimo has had seizures off and on since he was diagnosed fifteen years ago. However, since this last surgery, he hasn't had one.

"Y-yyeah—"

"I'll be right there. Hold on." I hung up and called the nurses' desk to let them know about the seizure, then grabbed my stuff and jumped in the car.

Kimo has been in the hospital for two months. He acclimated to the paralysis of his left side with stunning serenity, starting rehab after only a couple of days. The idea is to get moving as soon as possible and stick with it. The physical therapists say that he will be able to learn to stand and—probably—walk again. His left hand still can't move, but he has been working on lifting the arm. They say he has about a six-month window of brain plasticity wherein he can regain some range of motion.

But the real problem is, his head won't heal. The square of irradiated skin has refused to knit back together over the huge, C-shaped incision site, and so the back of his head is constantly leaking cerebrospinal fluid through the frankensteinian line of staples. There is always a damp spot on his pillow. The open wound means he is highly vulnerable to infection. He has had several lumbar drains to try and stop the leakage. He suffers an unending headache, which varies from a 6 to a 10 pain level. He is never not in pain. Yet every weekday, he happily wheels up to the rehab floor to practice standing up, taking tiny steps in between two metal parallel bars, slowly pushing wooden blocks from side to side with his arm. His left arm and leg are already shockingly withered from disuse. But every day, he gets up and tries again.

I burst into his room to find it empty. On his pillow and blankets, there is red tomato sauce flecked with bits of basil and tiny lumps of pasta. I remember that the seizures often cause him to vomit. *Where is he??* I race out into the hallway to the nurse's station.

"Kimowan McLain?? Where is Kimowan McLain?? Room 6044?" I make a strong effort not to scream at the gaggle of nurses.

"The artist?" says one young nurse.

"Yes, yes, the artist, the UNC professor." I crane my neck to see what papers they are looking at. "I just called. He was having a seizure."

"Yes, Mr. McLain has been moved to the ICU."

"Thank you so much. Can I see him."

"Only family members are allowed in the ICU."

"I am a family member." *I am the only family member.* These third-shift nurses don't recognize me. Laena flew back to the west coast two weeks after the surgery; before she left, we signed documents establishing us both as health care power of attorney. For the last two months—apart from the week

96

Baxter and I spent at Burning Man—I have been at this hospital every day.

A few minutes later I have my special ID and am walking through the massive double doors into the intensive care unit, which looks like a space station. Each patient lies in a kind of pod, surrounded by a wall of beeping machines and swarmed with different PICC lines and monitor cables. An ICU nurse tends to only one or two patients at a time—they stand at the ready, like soldiers, in every room.

I walk into Kimo's pod and see him laid out under the ICU's crushingly bright lights. His face is completely slack, eyes closed, mouth hanging open. He is slightly propped up in the bed, presumably to keep his airway clear. His breath rushes noisily in and out of his lax mouth. The nurse, a kind-looking blond man with a military haircut, explains to me in a low voice that the seizure was a bad one, that he is now in an unresponsive "postictal" state, which could last for days.

I walk slowly up to the side of his space-age bed, feeling his steady, loud breath move against my face. A clump of tomato sauce clings to his lower lip. I ask for a wet wipe and gently clean away the dried vomit. He doesn't move or open his eyes—he just continues to breathe heavily. If it weren't for his raspy breathing, he would appear to be dead.

* * *

He lies, completely inert, in the ICU for three days. Every day I come and watch him breathe through his hanging-open mouth. His lips dry out and chap and crack, large pieces of dead skin curling from them. The doctors have now understood that he has contracted bacterial meningitis, a life-threatening infection caused by the constantly leaking incision site. They have him on an antibiotic IV. On the third day, as I am sitting beside him looking into his empty face, his eyelids move.

"Kimo!" I blurt. His eyelids move again, opening the tiniest bit. "Hey..." I say, more quietly, taking his hand in mine.

His brown eyes suddenly open all the way, casting about the room for a few seconds before finding my face. "Hey, sweetie—" he says...faintly, but in his normal voice.

I can't and don't wish to stop the tears that spill over onto our clasped hands. "You were…gone for…quite a minute there." I squeeze his hand lightly. "I'm glad you're back."

"What happened?" he says, unalarmed, looking about the pod with a simple curiosity.

"You had a big, big seizure. You've been in here three days."

"Gawsh, three *days*?"

"Yes. This is the ICU."

"That's what I *thought*…" he says, taking his hand from mine to absently rub at his lips with one finger. Pieces of dried skin fall from them.

"You have…You've got meningitis, Hon."

"Aw, I fuckin *knew* it!" For weeks, he has been saying that his CSF smelled weird, that he knew he already had an infection. Of course, the doctors just blew him off. *The artist. The UNC professor.*

"They're giving you antibiotics."

"That's not gonna work," he says flatly. "It's been too long."

"I hope you're wrong," I reply, overjoyed to see his sharp opinions returning. "Anyway, they think that's what caused the seizure."

"Ah, jeez." He is looking more like himself by the second. The instant transition from living-dead-person back into my dear friend is staggering.

"We'll get you out of here soon, at any rate—"

"Yeah. This is *no* place to be—" and he widens his eyes comically, swooping his gaze around the room to take in all the spacepod details. By evening, he is back up on the neurosurgery floor, in a shared room with a quiet old man.

* * *

It's been a week since Kimo got out of the ICU. Though he has recovered from the seizure, the meningeal infection rages. The antibiotics, as he predicted, have done nothing. The incision keeps on leaking. The pain in his head has intensified, so that it now always hovers between 8 and 10. He can barely talk or eat; he can't read or sleep or watch movies on the computer. He often holds his right hand over his forehead, as though to shield it from pain. His eyes squint and close, squint and close. He can't go to rehab, he can't do anything. He just lies there, holding his head.

I show up, as usual, in the late morning, to check on things and bring him anything he needs. Today, when I walk in, he is staring out the window, his right hand on his forehead, his left hand lying useless on the thin white hospital blanket. When he looks over at me, I flash on the eyes of sick and injured street dogs in India—wild, hopeless, flat, expecting nothing beyond pain.

"Annie…" he says quietly, motioning me over.

"Yes, honey." I sit on the bed next to him, the clean white hospital sheets lightly scratching my legs. He leans close to me, his hand returning compulsively to his forehead.

"I don't want it," he says in an almost inaudible voice. Slowly, he shakes his head, *No.*

"What do you not want, sweetie?" He is still on the antibiotic IV drip, the thick white port shellacked with clear medical tape to his bruised forearm.

"This—" he says, spiraling his right hand to indicate the whole room. "Everything." He shakes his head again. He leans closer to me. *"I don't want it."*

"You don't want…*any* of this?" I ask. He has never spoken this way. He has always been eager to heal, hopeful, energized.

"No," he says, shaking his head with a bit more force, his voice hollow.

I look steadily into his eyes. The pain, the weeks of unrelenting pain. The savaged body. "I understand." I have committed to walking this path with him. I have committed to bearing witness. I will not look away. I will not let him be alone.

"It's just…" and his voice stops, as big, sudden tears pop into the corners of his eyes. He closes them.

"I understand," I repeat, never moving my eyes from him, even as he turns to look out the window again. Tears drip down the side of his face, wetting the already-damp pillow. *Two months ago we were dancing, underneath the warm rain.*

"Aaaahhhh," he cries, squeezing his eyes shut again.

The doctors have been talking about a last-ditch effort to stop the leakage and infection: going into the incision again (they have already attempted two skin grafts) and removing the flap of skullbone that has been sawn out of his head and put back in a total of three times. They reason that this repeatedly-detached bone flap is a vector for bacteria, and reassure us that they can go back in later and replace the missing piece of skull with a steel plate. They will bring in a plastic surgeon for additional skin grafting. I am beginning to realize that this is probably the only way he will survive.

XVII.

The Body

The ten thousand things are born of Being,
And Being is born of Non-being.

—Lao Tzu

The body, like the universe, is a single, unrepeatable miracle. You and only you will ever look out of your eyes…only you will ever know what it is like to walk this earth inside your body. The particular joys and fears and sorrows and ecstasies and pains that define your existence, only you will ever feel.

The body is born, the body dies. In between, the body sees, hears, touches, tastes, thinks, feels. Beyond this, we know almost nothing.

But we do know that the body is born into a universe that (on all observable scales) materially organizes itself in consistent and measurable ways. Our planet is (if you are SANE) a sphere. All other planets and stars are also spheres. These spheres revolve in ellipses, which are determined by gravity. What defines the non-quantum material realm is *roundness,* which is to say, *edgelessness.* The inescapably spherical shape of our own planet, as well as our dear sun, readily offer us a mini-metaphor for the shape—and hence, the nature—of the universe: what was once an irreducible center now expanding endlessly (for all intents and purposes) in all directions. And there is nothing we, with our meager human powers, can do to halt its expansion.

Through the dark lens of this metaphor—the sphere—we might get a glimpse into a different kind of knowing. We might come to understand that any center within a sphere is—for that object or particle—*the* center. We might gain a tiny scrap of insight outside the one-way railroad of time's arrow—in which we are trapped—and into the unimaginable beyondness that is the true context of our being. We might feel our tiny human mind begin to expand—perhaps in some way similar to how our universe is expanding.

What is beyond this beyond, we do not appear to—currently—have the capacity to know. What we do know, however, is that we are one of the ten thousand things born of being. And—without knowing what nonbeing is—we still may observe that being is born of nonbeing. The sphere is a symbol that can speak to such knowable and unknowable truths. We exist on the infinitely thin surface of a sphere that defines the observable, material universe. And there is also that illimitableness that exists both inside and outside the sphere, the without-whichness about which we might not have the wisdom to speak, but may—on occasion—sing.

XVIII.

December 30th, 1989

It has been almost a year since I heard the words stating that my father was dead. Since that day I have rushed forward, forward, into the future, and away from the place where it was possible that something so unbearably wrong could have happened. *But it did happen. He is gone.*

The daily pace of life since his funeral has stepped up into nonstop effort. I finished my spring semester with a 4.0; I am expecting a similar GPA when we get our fall semester grades in the mail any day now. I have three more weeks at home for winter break before I return to my routine in New York.

Steadily I have pruned all excess frivolities from my privileged life: gone are television, movies, parties, dates, pop culture, junk food, sweets, new clothes, makeup—anything I consider a shallow and foolish waste of time. My life bears no resemblance to the lives of the young students who surround me. I take little notice of them; I am focused at all times on my classes. Every afternoon, I run five miles in Riverside Park. For breakfast I eat a small bowl of crisped rice cereal with skim milk and a banana. Lunch is an apple, a huge coffee (with skim milk only), and an untoasted bagel with nothing on it. Dinner is black beans, couscous, and steamed broccoli. I do not drink alcohol or do drugs of any type, ever. I have not had a period in months, have no love interests or flirtations, and am wholly ignorant of and indifferent to the realities of sex and sexuality.

Every evening, I am in the library, reading for class, working on a paper, or studying for an exam. For "entertainment"—on a Friday or Saturday night when other students are out getting drunk and doing other things I can't and don't imagine—I walk from my front door at 120th Street and Claremont Avenue all the way down to the West Village, more than 100 blocks. If I am tired at that point, I take the subway back uptown. But often, I just turn around, and walk all 100 blocks again. I walk silently, wearing my glasses so I can see everyone and everything along the way. Safely within myself, I observe all the swirling, buzzing life that continues to take place just beyond me. It is comforting somehow. It is one of the very few things that is comforting.

Deep inside, I do not get past the constant swarm of *thinking about* my father's death. It is still a neverending distraction, a breathless reminder that must *ding...ding...ding* check in on itself to make sure that I remember this one unbearable truth that has altered everything forever: *Your father is dead. Your father is dead. He will never hug you again. He will never show up at the door, you will never hear his voice, you will never see his eyes smiling, never ever again.* I have to repeat repeat repeat these truths to myself in order to make them real, which feels like it has become—along with making straight A's—the task of my life. I must believe, I must make myself believe that he is really gone—gone from this life forever, and never ever coming back. It takes all my effort and it does not relent.

Since his death, my mother, brother, and I have been unable to speak my father's name to one another. His name, *Daddy*, seems to wait heavily at the bottom of a fathomless, dark pit that we will be vacuumed into should we dare to speak it. If referencing him is unavoidable, my mother will say, "your dad"; my brother will say "Pop." We rush through any mention of him, avoiding direct eye contact. "That book belonged to your dad." "I think Pop told me about that." We step carefully around him, around the fact of his ever having existed, and we do not speak, ever, of the constant, deafening, incomprehensible sound of his absence.

When I wake (at precisely 8 a.m., as always) at home on this Sunday morning, I realize that it has been years—many years—since I have made an appearance at my father's church, the Unitarian Universalist fellowship. I have not given Christianity a second thought since it evaporated into nothingness in the hours following his death, which still feels as though it has not actually occurred. I have a dull, drumming anxiety that this inability to make his death real—to *believe* it—indicates some kind of as-yet-undiagnosed mental disorder: an illness where people are discovered to be not quite full-blown sociopaths, but rather, simply insufficiently human: to lack the sensitivity and depth of heart to experience genuine humanity. *You didn't love him; how could you be human?*

I get dressed and eat a single slice of cheese toast with Mom, drinking two cups of coffee to quell any hunger pangs. Then, in the quiet, gray morning, I drive over to the UU. I do not even think of inviting Mom to come with me—this was *Daddy's* church. She still sporadically attends the same Presbyterian church where we were baptized. But I will never set foot in that church again. She never asks me to.

In the spare entranceway, a flurry of familiar faces sends a rush of warmth to my heart. Some come up to hug me—including original members of the church, back when it was just a few people gathered in someone's living room. I walk into the octagonal sanctuary to find a seat amidst the rows of folding chairs. I sit alone, a few rows back from the minister—this church's first—whom I haven't seen since my father's funeral.

She is young, with short light brown hair and piercing blue eyes like his. A few minutes into the usual Unitarian liturgy, she pauses. "Because today is...the last Sunday of the year," she says, her clear voice steady and full, "we are taking some time to acknowledge any members of our community, and their loved ones, who have...left us, in the last year." She pauses again and I shoot a glance down at my program, seeing the extra section added into today's service: "**Acknowledgment of Losses.**" She looks around the room, her gaze touching me briefly before she begins again: "So I now invite anyone among us who has lost a loved one, this year...to stand and share, share their name with us this morning."

My whole awareness is seized by a searing desire to speak my father's name, to acknowledge his death to this community he helped to establish. He rarely missed a Sunday service and donated many hours to the effort to purchase this land and build this very building we are sitting in.

I understand that I have to stand and speak his name today. It is up to me; I am the one who must speak his name.

A very elderly man wearing horn-rimmed glasses and a bright yellow cardigan stands first, mumbling the name of a relative in a strong Brooklyn accent. I can barely listen. My heart has begun to pound in anticipation of the task that lies before me. Yet, I am eager to fulfill this duty—I will, I *will* speak my father's name to this group of people he worshipped with for 12 years, people who knew and cared about him, who remember him as he was.

I am impatient as a portly middle-aged woman with gray hair and a purple tie-dye dress stands and speaks of the long illness of her mother, who must have died in her 90s—an age when you expect people to die. *My father shouldn't have died.* I'm restless, I want to stand and acknowledge him to this special gathering of people, I want to honor his name. I am ready.

As the gray-haired woman sits down, the minister's eyes seek my eager face. I half-raise my hand, meeting her gaze. She nods at me and I jump to my feet.

"I would like to acknowledge my father," I begin in a loud voice that booms through the quiet room, but stops short just before I get to his name—a name I haven't been asked to speak out loud for the last year. (*When did I last say my father's name?*) He's just been "my dad," or, "Pop," or, privately, in the sanctuary of my own mind, where I can still see and hear and touch him—*Daddy.*

Some quick force seems to have caught me by the throat, a dense mass I must—I *must*—push through in order to articulate my father's name: "Jim…Hhumphreys—" I try to continue, but the force presses urgently into my neck, like a fist pushing directly into my vocal cords but I will NOT, I will NOT, allow it to prevent me from acknowledging him, acknowledging the loss of him, which is so very impossible and yet happened, it happened, and it must be acknowledged because it was real; he is really gone from this earth never to return again, and I am the one who must speak this truth out loud today:

"…whhho was…a member…of this congregation—"

On the word *congregation* my voice shrieks itself up into an impossible highness and disappears as my throat closes entirely, because it must stop the aching leaden mass that is pushing, pushing, pushing suddenly to get out but that can't happen, I must complete my statement and honor my father's memory, it's the one responsibility I can fulfill, it is the one thing I can do, it is something I must do, I *have* to. I can't get enough breath in my lungs. My voice drops to a shamed whisper as I sputter out words of apology I hadn't planned to say, they push themselves out in a tight, hushed jumble, without will or volition: "…*andI'msorryIcan'tsayitproperly*."

My legs give out as an earsplitting, alien, animal wail hurls itself from some deep chasm within me and caroms sickeningly against the octagon of walls. As I fall backwards into my chair, the blatant, horrifying sound assumes a rhythm, ricocheting back to me from every angle as a pair of arms—it is my father's dear friend, Eunice—encircles me and begins to rock me, back and forth, back and forth, as I am powerless to stop the awful guttural ripping sounds that echo, echo, echo so humiliatingly everywhere in the silent room.

As from a sudden, great distance, I hear the low, collective gasp of everyone around me, they understand, I feel all their faces turning towards me, heavily, in sorrow—they feel so terrible for me and yet nothing can be done…nothing can ever, ever be done. They understand this, and I do not.

IXX.

It has been one year since Kimowan's head was sawn open for the third time, and it has been nine months since Baxter and I picked him and his new wheelchair up in front of the big automatic glass doors of the Neuroscience building to finally, finally bring him home. He spent two weeks in our extra room, wheeling around curious Vincent, instructing me stoveside on exactly how to fry pancakes, relearning how to be in a house again with half a body. After that brief crash course, he moved into a new apartment down the street with his closest brother, Luther, who has left his life in Calgary to come live here for a while.

Kimo's excitement to inhabit the new apartment has verged on ecstasy. Every day, he tends to some different corner of the place: organizing his art books and graphic novels just so, carefully arranging photographs on the fridge, taking hours to measure the exact length of fishing line required to suspend a perfectly round lavender glass bead one inch over the head of his Buddha sculpture, which sits serenely above the kitchen sink. He has made friends with the cardinals who come to his new bird feeder, spending whole afternoons on the back porch talking to them. Among them is an embattled, dominant male he calls "The Old Man." He sits and watches the young males taunt The Old Man, offering daily, steadfast encouragement between gentle puffs on his cigarette. "Hey, ignore those whippersnappers, man. You're the king!"

Though his insurance stopped paying for rehab a few months ago, he has continued to recover sensation and movement on his left side. The PTs told him that most people don't recover much movement after the first six months of rehab. But most people are not Kimo. He has invented a series of exercises he calls *kimo-chi*: a constantly changing variety of slow, repetitive motions. "Hey Annie," he will say, standing in the middle of his living room, legs splayed out wide for balance, "check it out!" And he will, slowly, hoist his thin left arm, its limp hand hanging, forward and up, forward and up. He makes slow, steady effort, day after day after day. And, week by week, the arm inches higher, and higher. He confesses to me one night that the most significant part of *kimo-chi* is when he takes time to gently stroke and kiss his limp hand and deadened arm and leg, leaning close and whispering to his hand, his foot: *Hey, I love you. It's gonna be okay.*

He gets a wooden cane and makes a video of himself dancing to a powwow drum track. He takes the cane and pounds it into the floor, following the drum's rhythm: *BAM…BAM…bam bam bam bam bam bam bam bam…* His left arm hangs at a slight right angle as his right arm pounds the stick into the floor. His mouth puckers in concentration. He sticks one foot forward, then the other, hokey-pokey style. He drops the cane and bends to get it in time with the music. He picks up the cane and cradles it in the crook of his right arm like a baby, stamping his right foot, then—a little more cautiously—his left. He videos himself talking to the birds, shaving with one hand, telling old Cree folktales about a trickster character named Wesakecak. When telling these old folktales to the camera, he wears a huge fake fur hat with pulled-down earflaps.

In his bathroom, there is a corner mirror: two mirrors conjoin at a right angle just over the sink, so that when you look directly into the corner where they meet, you see a Rorschach of yourself—one side reflected to look like two. Kimo realizes that he can stand at the edge of the perpendicular mirror and arrange his image so that he sees two right sides of himself…thereby allowing his brain to "see" a whole and balanced image of his body. He uses this mirror arrangement to "trick" his left side into sensing symmetry and movement: he will stand and move his undamaged right arm and hand, so that in the mirror both sides are moving. His left hand, hidden from the mirror view, sluggishly follows along. His brain, he reasons, seeing his body move, whole and integrated, then sends new recognitions and sensations to his left side, building new neurons and pathways. He continues to recover movement. A few months into this practice, we find an article in the *New Yorker* detailing a leading-edge research project that uses the exact same technique—called a "mirror box"—to help amputee patients overcome phantom limb sensations.

He gets new clothes—sweatpants that don't have to be buttoned or zipped, new white sneakers for walking outside, and, from the internet, a bunch of different kinds of hats: ballcaps, straw hats, knit beanies, and, his favorite—stingybrims. Hats, which he seldom wore before, are now an essential part of his daily ensemble—because, although none of his limbs have been amputated, a piece of his skull has.

After weeks of unceasing pain in the hospital, his incision still leaking and the infection raging, the doctors finally decided to operate and remove the large square "flap" of skullbone from the back of Kimo's head. I never knew before that someone could live without a piece of their skull. But out it went. They did some skin grafting, sewed him up, installed yet another lumbar drain, and—finally—his infection subsided, and the skin around his incision started to heal. He started to get better. The back of his head looks like a shark took a large bite out of it. I had imagined that he wouldn't look that different— that the brain would still mostly fill in the space where the skullbone had been. But it doesn't. The incision site just looks like a massive, melty dent, half-covered with weedy black hair. He tucks his hair behind his ears, plants his hat firmly, and heads out into the world, cane in hand.

* * *

Today is one of the hottest days of the summer. Today is also the first day of our second-ever hoop retreat, the same one we held last year when Kimo was in the hospital. Our guest list has quadrupled from 18 to 80. Increasingly over the last several months, Baxter and I have traveled all over the country teaching hoopshops—he leads the classes, while I walk around offering individual assistance. My hoop skills have sharpened dramatically; for the last two years, I've been hooping two hours a day, every day. Bax has just quit his bartending job so that we can travel and teach full time. Kimo is still on medical leave, but is scheduled to begin teaching again in January.

Our first event is a jam inside the large air-conditioned community center in the middle of town. I can't even hoop, I am hugging and talking to so many people. Everybody wants to know where Kimo is; the new tendrils of social media have connected us all; everyone has been following his journey back from death's door. Most of them have never met him.

One of the big doors on the other side of the room swings open, and I see first Kimo's brown cane, then his white sneakers, madras shorts, white tee, and pork pie hat enter the auditorium. I can see from here that he is wet with sweat. He sees me across the room and raises the tip of his cane in greeting—he can balance for minutes at a time without it. I run over to grab him a chair, but he isn't quite done yet; he wants to walk across the room and sit in front, on the stage. We walk, his left sneaker dragging softly across the shiny wood floor. People drop their hoops and cut through the crowd to us. "Kimo! *Kimo!!!*" He gingerly pauses to welcome the arms thrown around him from all sides, trying to hug back with his dangling left arm while holding the cane fast. His eyes keep cutting over to the stage, so I know he's tired. I pull him away from the gathering crowd, to the edge of the stage, where he sits down with a large exhale and a beaming smile.

"How'd you get here, Hun?" Though he is not officially allowed to drive yet, Kimo can easily maneuver his old white Honda with his strong right leg and arm, and takes it on tiny joyrides here and there.

He raises his cane. "Walked!" The distance from the community center to Kimo's apartment is about half a mile.

"You walked the whole way?" I can tell from his grin that it's true, but I'm still stunned—he hasn't walked anywhere near that distance in a year.

"Yep," he affirms, letting his gaze pan across the room. I can see that he has been planning this for a while.

"*Dude!*" I raise my palm and he smacks it.

A hooper who has admired Kimo online slinks up to get a photo with him. He cheerfully poses for a few shots while I go get him some water. When I come back, I see that he has stood up again, and someone has handed him a green and white striped hoop.

It still takes Kimo a full two minutes to stand up from the couch. He walks, but haltingly and with enormous focus and effort. It takes equal focus for him to lift his dangling left arm even a few inches. I haven't even wanted to ask him if he wants to try the hoop. I haven't wanted him to have any way to fail.

He holds the hoop in his right hand, "steering" it back and forth in time to the music. He has picked up Bluebird to dance like this a few times, but he has not tried to place the hoop around his waist and get it going, hula-hoop style. I have realized in the last year that the hula-hoop motion is very much like walking or running—you just need to be able to shift your weight, entirely and symmetrically, from one side of the body to the other. And Kimo's left side is still much, much weaker than his right.

But, all at once, he lifts the hoop up over his head, and brings it down around his body. He grabs it, as best he can, with both hands—taking extra seconds to carefully maneuver his left hand. He twists to the right, getting ready to throw the hoop left—he has always been a "lefty" hooper—keeping it nice and flat, and, *whoosh*…his intact right hand pushes the hoop into motion.

I'm afraid he's going to fall, but he doesn't; the hoop swings around once, twice; he's teetering a bit but it keeps going…it's wobbly but going, going…

"Hahaaaaa…" he says, looking at a spot somewhere beyond us, his arms chicken-winged above the whirling hoop. I bet he has been practicing without telling me. His smile sends a streak of light across the room.

He keeps the hoop going for a good two minutes before it drops.

XX.

Failure

Failure is an opportunity.

— LAO TZU

The hula-hoop taught me how to feel, and the hula-hoop also taught me how to fail—in the best possible way, which is to say, ostentatiously and repeatedly.

"If you never hear the sound of your hoop hitting the floor, you know you're not learning anything new," Baxter would often say to us, in those early days. After months and months and months of humiliating myself daily—often in the company of my world-class-hooper boyfriend—I began to get used to the sharp taste of failure, and how faithfully it precedes the incomparable sweetness of success.

I couldn't hula-hoop as a child because I couldn't tolerate the feeling of failure. The first time I encountered hula-hoops I was five years old. It was late afternoon, summer. My brother and I were at our babysitter's house with a group of other kids. She was an old woman who wore cotton housecoats, her long white hair pulled up into a french twist. Her home was a tiny cinderblock cottage on the edge of town where parents would drop their kids for hours at a time, sometimes all night (it was the 70s). In her verdant side yard, under the spreading oak tree, there was a sandbox and swingset, as well as piles and piles and piles of toys—including a stack of brightly-colored hula-hoops.

As several kids frolicked around the yard, someone picked up a hoop and started it around their waist. Instantly, every child flocked to the hoops, wanting to try. I watched my brother pick one up and...*whoop...whoop... whoop*...he got it going. Right away I began to itch for a turn myself.

After a minute or two, an abandoned pink hoop appeared on the grass below me. I grabbed it and set it around my waist, trying to move the way I had seen my brother do. It plopped right back down on the grass. My face growing hot, I picked it back up and looked again at my brother, at the bright hoop swinging...*whoop...whoop...whoop*...around him. I threw my hoop into rotation.

Plonk.

My tongue wedged itself between my back molars in humiliated frustration. I snatched the hoop up again and glanced around furiously at the kids surrounding me, their multicolored hula-hoops whirling around their waists without apparent effort. *What were they doing that I couldn't do?* I was the fastest runner in my class, boys included—I could climb to the top of the jungle gym! Again I released the hoop and tried the strange shimmying motion of the other kids.

Plonk.

I left the hoop there and stalked off to the swingset, angry tears stinging my eyes. And I did not touch a hula-hoop again until the day Kimo and I walked into Baxter's class, 30 years later.

* * *

In September of 2012, I started to write this book. I began with a different (terrible) title and some kind encouragement from a couple of my smartest friends. I spent the next six months writing the first draft.

Through a generous miracle, I caught the interest of a powerful agent in New York, who matter-of-factly informed me that what I had

114

written was not a book, but rather a meandering and incomplete yet interesting idea. She immediately grasped, however, the kind of book I *wanted* to write. So I set about trying to write that book. I wrote a second draft. It didn't work.

2014, I wrote another draft. It also didn't work.

In 2015, I completed another draft, which failed.

I wrapped up the next draft in the summer of 2016, feeling like I had broken through! THIS was the version! YES! This is what I had wanted to say! I promptly swooshed it off to the agent.

She responded by breaking up with me.

In 2017, I wrote another draft. It was a pile of shit.

2018. Another year, another draft. Another. Total. Failure.

In 2019—between long Saturdays of protest, standing opposite a mean gaggle of Confederate-flag-waving goobers angry at the removal of one of their statues from the public square—I decided to try my hand at a seventh version. The seventh version is this book.

XXI.

March, 2009

I'm lying on my stomach on the floor of Kimo's apartment, paging through his *Jimmy Corrigan: The Smartest Kid on Earth* graphic novel. Vincent lolls nearby. It's past midnight. I've been here since early evening. Every couple of weeks, a group of us meets here for supper—a small group of friends who have been helping Kimo navigate his post-op treatments, which include both radiation and chemotherapy. We also investigate clinical trials to see if there is one he might be able to join, and talk through the pros and cons of every health-related decision he must make. And we cook and eat and talk and laugh for hours at a stretch.

Bax usually comes, along with my bff Ali, our friend Thomas, dear hoopfriends Beth and Bonnie, and our newest hoopfriend, Antje, Kimo's speech therapist from the hospital. After meeting us all she became fascinated by hooping, and started attending Baxter's class. She has also struck up a friendship with Kimo, who charmed and delighted everyone he came in contact with at the hospital. A couple of months after he got home, he told me—wearing his impish grin—that Antje was coming over for tea.

"Awesome!" I replied heartily. "She's so great."

"She is," he said, half-hiding his mouth behind his hand. "She's coming *Tuesday*."

"Excellent."

"I really kinda…" He trailed off for a second, hand still shading his mouth.

I looked over at him, his lips smirking up behind his hand. "What?" I said.

"I have a kind of a *crush* on her," he confided in a dramatic whisper.

A cold sensation trickled through me. I couldn't, I just couldn't let him get too caught up in this. "Well, she *is* really beautiful…" I said neutrally, ignoring the hope in his eyes, hoping he'd understand what I could never say: *You're pushing 50, half-paralyzed, missing a quarter of your skull, and dying of cancer; she's twenty years younger and gorgeous, she could have anyone she wanted.*

Ever since then, they have gotten together for tea every few weeks, and Antje has folded right into our ad hoc medical-advocacy group. She is willowy and tall, with dark blond hair and brown eyes, and a sly, quiet humor. She is also attentive and careful, her German sensibilities showing up in her facility with detail. Her familiarity with the hospital helps keep us attuned to how different treatments and trials might affect Kimo. I'm deeply touched that she has come to care so much about him.

Everyone else left earlier this evening—Antje and I are the only remaining guests. Bax went home to hoop. Luther moved back to Canada a month or so ago. Kimo is sitting at his computer in a straw hat, glasses slightly askew, dj-ing us through a course on obscure Canadian 80s bands. "Awh, these guys,"—he says, swiveling around and raising one finger aloft—"Back in Edmonton, we used to just dance the *hell* outta this song!" He bobs his head to the weird, tissuey rock & roll I cannot imagine dancing to.

"I don't get this Canadian rock," I report from the floor. "Why does it sound so…*muffled*?"

"Better than German rock," deadpans Antje from the kitchen.

On cue, Kimo and I erupt in guffaws. Earlier we shared a toke from his glass-blown bowl. Antje doesn't smoke weed, but sips periodically from a tiny glass of red wine.

"So, I was thinkin'," Kimo says when we stop laughing, "You know how everybody is always saying 'Oh, we're so addicted to *oil*'?"

"Well, we are," I respond.

"That's what I'm saying!" he says excitedly. "It's not the oil!"

"It's not?" Antje and I exchange looks.

"No," Kimo says, at once utterly calm and in full professor mode. "It's not the *oil* we're addicted to…" He raises his right hand again, all his fingertips drawn together, pointing. "It's the *speed*."

We pause in silence for a moment.

I reply simply, "It is."

Antje comes around the open countertop and plonks down on the carpeted floor between me and Kimo. She leans against the bookcase and raises her arm to look at her watch. "OH, Lord…" she says, the Southern exclamation sounding natural in her mouth. She's been in the States for several years.

"What time is it?" I know it must be late. Since Bax and I have started our traveling life, I don't really have a bedtime unless we are on the road and have a workshop in the morning.

"One," she answers, looking somehow sheepish.

"DANG!" I declare. "I thought it was only like midnight."

"I *wish* it was midnight," she says in a playful whine, rolling her head back and forth against the book spines. "I've got to be at work in the morning."

"What time?"

"Seven."

"Oh my god!" I exclaim. "What time do you have to get *up?*"

"Probably, like six."

"*Six!*" I shout, my mind suddenly racing. Because, she's only got five hours to *sleep* and she's still got to drive home, which is like fifteen minutes, and get ready for bed and then drive back in the morning, she must *want* to be here, she must be staying here on purpose! My stomach curls and my face flames in a startle of embarrassment: *I'm* the interloper, here! They're waiting for me to leave!

I scan through a couple more pages of *Jimmy Corrigan* as camouflage. I need to feign tiredness and get out of here *ASAP.* In the lull, Antje stands to look over Kimo's shoulder at an animated graphic of the color wheel. I notice how close she is to him, how she leans down so that her face is right next to his.

"Well, I gotta get to bed, guys," I sigh with manufactured fatigue, forcefully slapping the graphic novel shut. I stand and they turn in unison from the computer, their silent huge eyes and not-quite smiles confirming that this decision is in all our best interest. I hug them both, call Vincent, and head to the front door. Before shutting it I turn around. "Night, y'all," I call, raising my hand to wave. From their cozy corner, they wave back, indulgently, like kind grandparents, touched and amused by the vain oblivion of youth.

XXII.

The Tao

There was something undifferentiated and complete
Which existed before heaven and earth.
Soundless and formless,
it depends on nothing and does not change.
It operates everywhere and is free from danger.
It may be called the mother of the universe.
I do not know its name; I call it Tao.

— LAO TZU

Stuck to my father's refrigerator, for as long as I can remember, was a single-panel comic cut out from a newspaper. It depicted a squat man standing at the edge of a deserted island, flanked by a lone palm tree, looking eagerly up into the sky at a single, shimmering star. The caption below said, *Well, I'm a lifelong Unitarian—but what could it hurt to make a wish?*

I like and embrace the hula-hoop as a spiritual symbol precisely because it draws attention to the very absurdity and arbitrariness of that choice. We, as beings, wander about in the dark labyrinth of conscious embodiment until—as Galileo observed—we find a metaphor that illuminates something about our position within the heart-stopping unlikelihood of our ever having come to exist at all. What I appreciate and celebrate about the circle—and its mother, the sphere—is that it communicates to me specific and useful truths of which I am spiritually in need. At the same time, neither the hula-hoop nor the circle nor the sphere require me to submit to them as gods, or wrap myself in a mantle of dogma, or divorce myself from the experiences of my body and my senses...ever, at all.

Before I found the hoop, I was marooned in a merely literal world. There were only three dimensions, tied together by a single, historically traceable storyline of truth. There was nothing in this model to allow me to feel a sense of awe sufficient to the miracle of existing. Though I had outgrown my childhood religion within a span of minutes, I never outgrew my human need of the spirit's search for meaning, the piercing drive to come into relationship to that which gave rise to me, to us, to our glorious mother, this earth, to the infinite firmament that surrounds us, on every conceivable side.

Once my father disappeared into somewhere beyond our shared, physical world, that world—the one he had disappeared *from*—had to become my spiritual starting point. At that time, it was an asymbolic place, a vacuum to be filled with the kind of verifiable information found in libraries and universities. I spent years there, inscribing lines upon lines of text into my personal archive, adding more and more stories to the existing narrative that comprised the life story I was always, always, always writing. But it wasn't enough.

It wasn't enough because I am a human being, and as such I am in need of relationship to the unknown and the unknowable. As a human being, I require a way to connect to that which exists beyond me, beyond what I can see and know and hear and feel with my own hands (which is, actually, just about everything).

What I needed was a metaphor that could unite the subjective and objective worlds in a single and uniquely graceful stroke. I needed an image that could represent both the unplumbable mystery that is the Unseeable, and the accurately measurable physical realm in which we— during our human incarnation, (which is, incidentally, happening, as always, *right now*)—exist.

I needed a shape—not a theory, not a word, not a story, not a character—but a palpable *thing* that could translate to me the dynamic of Time, of Space, of Motion...of that irreducible material world in which we live every single second of our human lives—traditionally represented by the often arcane languages of physics and math.

I needed an organizational symbol by which to navigate my spiritual journey: a symbol that could apply to everywhere and everything, that explicitly included my vanished father, that could reliably function—every single minute of every day—as radically uniting, simple, self-evident, and true.

I needed a channel for the overwhelming experience of conscious embodiment: a way to bring my entire being—body, mind, and spirit—into the same moment, into that which in meditation is often called *the present*.

I needed a way to define to myself both the Alpha and the Omega, the beginning and the end, the Inner and the Outer, the physical and the nonphysical, the everything and the nothing, what we know and what we do not know, the fullness and the emptiness, the immeasurably vast and the unimaginably small, the Yin and the Yang, the good and the bad, the inevitable darkness and the equally inevitable light, infinity and zero, form and formlessness, now and eternity, earth and sky, sun and moon, here and there, life and not-life, the totality and its opposite, which a poet once called

nothing that is not there and the nothing that is.

And all these things that had eluded me I found in the most unlikely—indeed supremely absurd—of ways: by dancing with a cheap, ungodly, plastic, ridiculous, simple, foolish, brightly-colored hula-hoop, wrapped in shiny tape.

(But—seriously, though).

XXIII.

July 29th, 2011

I'm in a large rented gymnasium in a small, picturesque town in Bavaria. I've been traveling all day to get here in time for the first-ever European Hoop Convention, where I will be one of the featured instructors. Since Baxter and I broke up two years ago, I've been traveling and teaching on my own.

Our breakup was one of those fabled, loving, beautiful breakups you think never really happens. Yet, it did happen. We had been together around the clock for almost four years—living together, working together, traveling together, hooping together, spending barely a minute apart. But the closer we became as community leaders and friends, the further apart we grew as lovers. And because sex has always been the most difficult and least self-evident thing in my life, this separation—in hindsight—has seemed inevitable.

We both managed, by some unwilled intervention of grace, to recognize our predicament in the same moment. For days, we held each other and cried, promising to give each other enough space and time to allow our bestfriendship to continue unimpeded. We made a vow not to see each other for several weeks. We agreed on a contingency plan that we could text each other whenever necessary, and talk on the phone after two weeks. We adhered to all of our agreements. We did not see each other in person for five weeks. When we finally saw one another again, we were best friends—and we have remained so to this day.

Kimo and Antje (who he calls "AJ") moved in together a few months after I finally took note of their budding romance. They moved her brightly painted upright piano and cats and all his books and precious objects into a rental house at the elbow of an L-shaped street, just a couple of blocks away from the co-op. They filled the house with artwork and planted a big garden. Kimo kept teaching and writing blogs and making videos. He learned how to use an electric scooter, zooming to and from the co-op at will. She continued working at the hospital, helping people learn how to speak again, while keeping all his therapies, medications, appointments, and checkups organized and in flow. They laughed together. A lot. He got a ring and asked her to marry him. She said yes.

But they haven't had a chance to actually get married. Because a few months ago, he started having seizures again. A lot of them, one after the other. His movement deteriorated, his words began to slur. He had to rely more and more on his electric scooter for mobility. More scans confirmed what we already knew: the tumor was growing again.

In April they made the quick decision to move up to Alberta, to be near Kimo's mother, auntie, and other family. As soon as they arrived, he took another turn for the worse. They never even moved their stuff into an apartment—Kimo was admitted to a small hospital in St. Cloud, where he has been receiving only palliative care.

I flew up to see them in June, stopping at the Than Than Noodle House in Edmonton to bring his favorite dish ("The red soup!") to the hospital. He ate it all, with relish. Antje and I piled in bed with him to watch episode after episode of "The Osbournes." She took a nurse's pinafore and draped it over her head, in perfect imitation of a nun's habit. She grabbed a cross from the wall and started babbling in tongues, dowsing the cross over everything, faking Latin prayers, breaking us up with giggles—Kimo's laugh still rushing delightedly from his drooping mouth.

Every night since they arrived at the hospital, Antje has slept on the floor of Kimo's room. She has made a little pallet in the kitchen alcove, so she can hear him if he ever calls out in the night. The hospital is tiny and intimate—when a woman is giving birth down the hall, you can hear her cries clearly. And, later on, the quavering cries of her baby. Kimo loves to hear the new babies being born. When he is napping (which he does several times a day), Antje rushes down the hall to a conference room, where piles of Kimo's artwork wait to be archived. She carefully spreads out each piece on the large table, then handwrites a number and description in a large ledger. The Smithsonian's National Museum of the American Indian has requested his entire body of work.

Just before I left for this five-week European tour, I flew back up to Alberta again. I asked Antje what I should bring. "Anything good to eat, with color, and flavor," she said, adding, "He misses the flavor." I went to the upscale food store in Edmonton and got cured meats, cheeses, fresh-baked bread, butter. Beet salad, wild rice salad, green beans. Cream for their coffee. Chocolate. I arrived with bursting bags, shoving what I could into the little dorm-style fridge, spreading out the best things on his large rolling bed-tray. Kimo was weaker, not talking much, his hair slick and greasy, the left side of his face sagging like a stroke victim's. But he ate from every container.

His arms and legs, like my father's, had grown sticklike. His face was swollen from steroids, like my dad's had been. The left side of his body flaccid, inert, pulled down by gravity—the right side shrunken down, withered. No fear in his face, his body. Him gazing with unbroken love at Antje, whom he calls "my sweetie pie." Hugging me with his weak right arm, gazing at pictures of Vincent and Baxter, greeting his mother and auntie with his now-lopsided grin. His laugh quieter, his throat always sounding half-clogged. Clearing his throat again, weakly. Dropping into another nap, head rolling back on the pillow, puffy eyes closed, mouth open.

* * *

The convention coordinator, a fastidious young German woman, shows me to my "room": a large storage closet on the far side of the gym, which I will be sharing with two other teachers. Tall stacks of blue gym mats will serve as beds. "Is there a pillow? Or any blankets?" I ask. She seems startled by my questions and bustles out to find something. I missed the dinner hour and there were no leftovers, so I've just been eating hazelnut cookies and fruit. I'm angry with myself for being annoyed. I know they are operating on a shoestring budget. I climb up on top of one of the huge blue stacks, lie down on my stomach, and log onto the wireless network.

I haven't spoken to Kimo or Antje since I saw them three weeks ago; I have been checking in on them via Facebook, where Antje posts regularly and we exchange messages.

I open the app and immediately see the post on Kimo's page. But I don't believe it at first because—someone would have called me, right? Someone would have messaged me...*my friend, my brother*...but I can see that it's public, I see all the comments, it's real now, no one called me *it's not about you* but it has to be real because there it is in full view of the world, and so have to I see—again—my foolish vanity. *My brother, my only Kimowan.*

And I brace myself, expecting the unbreachable gate to slam down between us—between me and my intrusively real body, still here, always still here...and the fact of my friend: his sweet roguish face, twisted body, singularly powerful mind, and bright clear brown eyes, which looked on me with only approval. *He's gone.*

I must not move or make a sound, for there is nothing where he was—he was here with us, he was here. I must not move or make a sound because I must know that he is gone (I do not say *he's dead*—I do not say this, even to myself). I must understand that it has happened, it is real now, it is more real than anything else could be. *He's gone.* I have to make it real to myself, I *have* to—I will not slip into the nothingness of denial. *I will not cringe away, I will believe.* And as I apply this thought like a scalpel, I feel not the nothing that is not there, but something that is.

I feel the convex surface of our visible, tangible world as it pushes out from nothingness into material reality—how this, our apprehendable dimension, is like the surface of a perfect sphere: that realm we can see, feel, hear, taste, touch, which pushed itself outward from a sheer context of notbeing. I feel how this manifest surface meets us at the perfectly angled pitch described by one of the sphere's infinite radii, as it endlessly expands from an immeasurably infinite inner point. And as I feel this surface, how wonderfully *comprehensibly* the image of the sphere describes it, I feel something else, which is everything behind, within, throughout, beyond it.

He is right here, I suddenly realize, looking at the empty space next to me. *He is just on the other side of that neverending angle.* I see my friend's sweet, curious face now; I feel his presence throughout my whole being. Because I can now feel how, just on the other side of the seamless convexity we experience as embodied life, there is everything that gives rise to that convexity: the infinite innerness that lies at the heart of our planet, our sun, our own bodies—and the illimitable expansion that issues forth from each center. There is the manifest world, I suddenly realize, and there is everything unseen that abuts, surrounds, exists with, and gives rise to it. All that dark matter, all that invisible space, all that we can neither see nor measure, is exactly that which invisibly supports—from every imaginable angle—the seeable, touchable surface on which we live. *He's not gone...he is right here. He is right here beside me—within that concavity that is not-us, inside the exact inversion of everything we can touch: safely, right next to me, on that other side.*

Dali's Duckmeat and Old Suit Enchilada

— a dream-poem by
Kimowan Metchewais

Make a big bowl of bread stuffing
Fry sliced duck meat, skin and fat
Mix everything together and add favorite vegetable chunks
Buy a man's secondhand suit
Cut out a one-foot square of the most worn fabric
Line the fabric with butter and herbs
Add fresh chunks of avocado to mix
Put mix on fabric square, tuck ends and roll
Deep fry for three minutes
Let cool
Place enchilada snugly under left arm
Walk around town
Yum.

XXIV.

Postscript: 2021

You higher men, the worst about you is that you have not learned to dance.... What does it matter that you are failures? How much is still possible!

— Friedrich Nietzsche

Yesterday—two months after some of those same Confederate-flag-waving goobers I mentioned earlier stormed our Capitol, causing the death of five people—I went up into my attic to check a leak. Of course, while I was up there, I could not help rummaging around in some of the open boxes I quickly shoved upstairs more than ten years ago, when I moved out of this house to live in New York again and travel the country with Vincent. Many of the boxes I've had a chance to go through since I moved back in 2013—but some, I haven't.

I popped open a bright red metal tea tin painted with circus imagery to find a tiny treasure trove. An infinitely small plastic tea set in a clear plastic case no bigger than a matchbox. A miniscule pair of plastic palm trees. Colorful cutout affirmation quotes a hooper used to pass out at retreats. Minute editions of fairy tales with stamp-sized pages. And I found a couple of tiny and precious pieces of my friend in there—pieces I had almost forgotten.

Kimowan had created—along with our dear friend Gord—a series of written meditations they called *Zen Satan*. They wrote "fortunes" on scraps of paper, rolling each one up individually and placing them inside cellulose capsules, like little pills of art. I found my favorite one:

Hope, that plastic carrot replete with synthetic scent hung before the nostrils of an ass to be led up a mountain and off a cliff! Where does it come from?

One of the stated missions of Zen Satan was to go beyond oppositionality—to challenge the assumption of a binary world, in which only two positions are possible: For and Against. The name itself speaks to this ambition. And this quote speaks to the unexpectedly thrilling resilience of hope, which refuses to be vanquished, despite our increasing attempts to corner and beat it to death with our certainties.

* * *

When my father died in 1989, the internet had not yet been introduced to the public. It would be, only one year later. He never sent a single email or received a text message. I don't think he ever touched the keyboard of a computer.

Kimo loved the awe-inspiring power of the internet and created his own website, www.kimowan.com, in the long months after his brain surgery. It was, unsurprisingly, a thing of great beauty, featuring not only his clean, conversational sentences, but also an irreplaceable collection of special images—photographs, artwork, song lyrics, remnants of his artistic PROE-cess (listen...I still have to make fun of his accent), which he believed in and lived with every quark and gluon of his being.

Of the internet, he wrote: *As people join this web, each establishing a new singularity of existence, another point, another center, there comes a realization that we cease to be points somewhere on an evermore intricate matrix, but we are more like a particle in the fuzz, a pixel in the static blur—except, while each of us is a molecule in the cloud, we are also each a cloud, or at least the small turbulence that set off the storm and produced a cloud.*

But, he asks himself, *where was I in all this? Was I just a point somewhere on this ball? Yes, and no.*

The title of this entry is *Finding a Quantum Self.* He goes on to compare the embodied self to a fixed star in an observable galaxy. And yet, he contends, the internet is not like a star—or a body—and does not behave like one:

The problem with this metaphor and others like it, is that it names a place. To him, the distinction is clear: *Since we resist the unplace, the abstract, we make metaphors of secure place, things with breadth, width and height: a spider's web, a bolt of cloth, tangle of hair, jar of beads.*

He was losing his body, his place in the universe. His tangle of shiny black hair. His jar of beads.

There is no edge in the internet, he muses. *There might be clusters, people who appreciate photography, hula hoopers, fans of Herzog, but those are not places.* He was aware that the body is a place. He continues: *…if these clusters are not defined enough to be place, they are occupied simultaneously by other quasi-places. It seems impossible that two points could occupy the same space, but that is what happens on the internet.*

There is an indisputable edge to one human body. It is the size of a person, the shape of a man. It has the eyes of an artist. The hands of an inventor. Brain of a poet. Heart of a brother.

The internet is a thought, Kimo wrote. *It either is or is not. There is no such thing as a half thought.* He had almost exactly one hundred weeks left to live in his body.

Here on the internet, he wrote, *we each exist. We are on.*

He is here now, with us, within reach.

We are a planetary hum, Kimo wrote, *for as long as no one trips over the cord.*

* * *

Today, the existence of truth itself is under siege. Instead of a central and comfortingly definable shared truth, we split and split and split off, like bubbles, into tinier and tinier clusters of agreed-upon information. The mission of Zen Satan to break down the binary once and for all could never have foreseen what a strange place we find ourselves in right now.

But we are in a place. We are here. It is now. We are embodied. If you are reading this, you have a body.

Even if much or most of your body doesn't work—like Kimo's or my father's at the end—you have a body. This information I am sharing is passing into your consciousness through a portal that is irrefutably housed within one specific human body: yours.

Just as no spin exists without a polarity, no consciousness—such as we know or understand this phenomenon, which is to say barely—exists without a body.

And the story of the body is real; the subjective and lived experience of the endless razor-wire loop of racism is real; the infinite trespasses felt by a female or femme body are all real; the incidental insults that differently abled people sustain are real; the subtle and blatant bigotry that gay and trans and nonbinary people endure daily is real.

And white privilege is real; structural and institutional white supremacy is real; the architecture that upholds white dominance, police brutality, and the unending terrorism of Black people is real. The story of whiteness—which, despite being a myth, has caused so much real violence, torture, and death—is a story about *the body*.

Though our spiritual context remains infinitely infinite—encompassing as it must everything that exists and might be hypothesized to exist—our stories are told through the frailty and folly of our human bodies. Every story that is told is told through the singularity of one human body. And every single body will tell the same story differently.

This plain fact points to another element that has proved as irreducible as the fact of spacetime curvature: the observer effect. In physics, the inescapable role of the observer—be it human, mechanical, or theoretical—always alters the outcome of the equation.

For us—embodied, living human beings—there is a specific locus of this observer. It is the human body. *Your* body. The only one you will ever have. Each of us will only ever have one body—a singularity, a unique and transitory point within the infinite context of spacetime.

George Floyd had only one body, which was sadistically and unforgivably stolen from him. Today is the second day of his murderer's trial.

* * *

I wrote this book because our stories of our subjective, lived experiences have value and are essential. If we did not believe in the value of subjective experience, we would not believe in racism—we would not believe our Black friends and family when they tell us of being followed, being called hideous and degrading names, being targeted and brutalized.

We would not believe in sexism or sexual assault: we would not believe our daughters, girlfriends, wives, sisters, aunts, mothers, grandmothers, when they tell us of the rapes they have survived…far too many than we could ever allow our minds to imagine. We would not listen when Black, Brown, Indigenous, Asian, or Latinx loved ones share their stories of being profiled, harassed, silenced, dismissed. We would ignore our disabled neighbors and friends when they try to confide in us about living in a world built for the able-bodied. We would brush away the stories of our queer siblings, our trans beloveds, our nonbinary family members.

I wrote this book because I believe that our subjective feelings—our *emotions,* those powerful sensations that move within us—are an intrinsic part of the endlessly undulating mosaic that is reality. I believe they are our teachers; they show us who we are by allowing us to experience what we feel and what we want. I believe that the practice of self-knowledge is not possible without the human experience of *feeling.*

And I wrote this book because it was my hula-hoop that taught me how to feel. I believe what the self-help cheesers say: *feeling is healing.* I have found it to be true, myself. Within my own human body. I have (finally) understood that *feeling* is not *thinking*…they are distinct phenomena. They might inform one another, but they are not one in the same thing. I needed this understanding; it has helped me to live more authentically, and to suffer less.

I wrote this book because everyone deserves to suffer less—especially those most directly and brutally impacted by the pernicious divisions and inequities we live with under a capitalist system that runs on the explicitly evil fuel of white supremacy. But even the white supremacist weirdos who doxx me online and threaten me in the streets deserve to suffer less. I know that they are suffering, as we all are. I believe that dancing is one thing that can help heal suffering for anyone living inside a human body (which is everyone reading this).

And I wrote this book because I was unreconciled to space and time; I did not understand what these things were; I did not comprehend my existential condition; I did not know where my father had gone when his body stopped breathing more than three decades ago. I needed to understand this, yet I had no way to. The hula-hoop...the circle—and its mother, the sphere—gave me a way.

* * *

At the center of your being you have the answer: you know who you are and you know what you want.

—Lao Tzu

The center of my being is a physical place; it exists; it is something I can feel. It is a place I can sense with my embodied, proprioceptive, subjective faculties, which are unfairly maligned means of experiencing reality. That revelation, which came to me through the spiraling conduit of the hula-hoop—the revelation that *I feel, therefore I am*—could not have so effectively or efficiently reached me any other way. It is a strange and wonderful miracle that arrived on a magic carpet of heartbreak, friendship, cannabis sativa, and boy-craziness.

Why do all people smile when they first try to hula-hoop? Why do people smile and laugh while loudly protesting over and over that they "can't do it"? Why do all people experience delight the first time they "get" it, feeling the hoop go around a few times? Why are some people so shocked by this delight? Why are some people so shocked to learn that our bodies, in certain ways, know more than we do?

The hula-hoop reminds us of the embodied intelligence that we have all possessed since birth. And, significantly, it reminds us that we know how to use this embodied intelligence—we have always known, since before we even understood how to think.

The hula-hoop—at a time when I needed it most—invited me back inside my body, and taught me how to dance. Not to dance a choreographed routine for an audience in full costume and makeup, but to dance for the sheer untouchable joy of being alive. The hula-hoop reminded me of my humanity—something that might seem insignificant, unless you have believed yourself at times to be other than human.

* * *

I define hoopdance as: any possible flowing combination between body and hoop. This definition allows for all existing possibilities, as well as those which have not yet been discovered. I call this image The Infinite Sphere.

In the center of the Infinite Sphere stands the dancer. Her body, her mind, her whole soul and spirit. And emanating out from this center are all possible trajectories her body might create with the hoop. The Infinite Sphere represents all the possible shapes that may be created, all possible rhythms and combinations, all possible dances. The dancer is free, at any moment, to turn in any direction, to shift the direction of her hoop, to adapt to any change in her environment, to express something new, to try something never-before-thought-of. Within the matrix of the Infinite Sphere, it is always possible for her to make a new, and different, choice.

And this skill, outside the hoop, is one she might find quite likely to benefit her, if she is in Flow: in that state of constant recognition that every moment—every single moment of every minute of every hour that passes us by, never to return—is unique.

And yet: there is a boundary: there are immutable laws of physics that proscribe the limitations of this, and of any, dance form—and of any form, really. The hoop is a limit, an edge, a containment of experience that is rendered perceptible through being a specific Thing, rather than everything-all-at-once. It is a metaphor of our universe, and of our experience within it.

One way we can learn how to find the one and only, never-to-be-repeated present is through embodied practice. You might find it through swimming, cycling, woodworking. You might find it through fly-fishing, yoga, running, rowing, surfing, jumping rope, t'ai chi, skydiving, dancing tango, throwing pots, whittling, skateboarding, playing guitar. You might find it walking your dog on a muddy path beside a creek in the early evening. You might find it in the chant you repeat until it resonates through all the layers of your being: the irrefutable body, the lonely mind, the deepening heart, the ever-expanding spirit.

You might find it while lifting heavy weights. You might find it in prayer. You might find it through the simple act of hammering a nail. You might find it while singing. You might find it any time you are entering your body and using it towards a single purpose in a single moment: bringing together all those layers of being into that moment, just now, which as we speak about it has already passed—that ever-escaping place we have only the words to call *the present.*

And if you're very, very lucky—more lucky than anyone could ever possibly imagine—you might find this place inside the curve of a circle made out of cheap plastic PVC tubing, covered with the softest stretchy leopard-skin fabric, wearing a torn-up sheet over your face, listening to India Arie, crying, while your future best friend tells a fairy tale that means the world to you will never be closed, will never be a place without play and discovery, ever again.

Seriously, though.

Works Consulted

Campbell, Joseph. *The Inner Reaches of Outer Space*. New World Library, 2002.

De Botton, Alain. *The Consolations of Philosophy*. Penguin, 2001.

De Botton, Alain. *Religion For Atheists*. Vintage, 2012.

Hawking, Stephen. *A Brief History of Time*. Bantam, 1988.

Jung, Carl Gustav. *Memories, Dreams, Reflections*. Pantheon, 1963.

Kingston, Maxine Hong *The Woman Warrior: Memoirs of a Girlhood Among Ghosts*. Knopf, 1976.

Van Gogh, Vincent. *Dear Theo: The Autobiography of Vincent Van Gogh*. Penguin, 1995.

Walker, Evan Harris. *The Physics of Consciousness*. Basic Books, 2008.

Wilczek, Frank. *A Beautiful Question: Finding Nature's Deep Design*. Penguin, 2015.

Acknowledgements

First and foremost and always, I thank my parents, Grace and Jim, for raising us to be weird artists who care. I thank my brother Greg for being my creative inspiration since birth, and my sister-in-law, nephew, and niece for completing our family.

I also thank my extended family—the Strains, Bensons, Lintons, Rockafellows, Kitchens, & Helmboldts—for their steadfast support and love.

My gratitude for my hoop brother Jonathan Livingston Baxter can never be measured. And I honor and thank my hoop mothers, Vivian "Spiral" Hancock and Julia "Julah" Hartsell, sine qua non.

I honor the memories of my hoop dancestors, known and unknown--especially our first contemporary flowart hoopdancer, Anah "Hoopalicious" Reichenbach. And I honor the worldwide hoop community, those incredible people who have been brave enough to take the leap through awkwardness into joy, inspiring the rest of us to come along.

This book would never have come into being without the loving help of my dearest Pea, Ariane Conrad, and our brilliant friend, Dalton Conley. Thank you both for your belief in me.

I thank my teachers, particularly those who encouraged my writing: Jean Ashley, James East, Martha Higginbotham, Ruth Krouskup, Robert G. O'Meally, Celeste Schenck, Mary Gordon, Mark Rudman, Tony Hoagland, Carl Phillips, Renate Wood, Michael Ryan, and Mary Leader.

Respect and gratitude to my dear colleagues and skilled friends who in specific ways helped make this manuscript into a book: Emilie White, Ian Wilson, Sydelle Kramer, Belle Boggs, Tristan Copley Smith, Brecken Rivara, Sally Torchinsky, Kubra Coltrane, Anna Norwood, Ashley Brown, Jennifer Ho, April Jennifer Choi, Khan Wong, TZ Rogers, Nicole Wong, Em Robbins, Laura Scarborough, Kara Donovan, and Nuria Lunallena.

And my love and thanks to the special people whose support and belief sustained me over the eight years it took to write this book: Claire-Elisabeth Hartman, Ali Gunn, Tricia Mickelberry, Elana James, Tain Collins, Kane Lopinski, Ian Williams, Marcia Julien, Ariana Vigil, Anna Blackshaw, Tim McKee, Michelle Nayeli Bouvier (special thanks for "second favorite direction"), and my Justice Family in Alamance County, in particular Sylvester Allen.